Praise for S

How do you have compassion for a student sitting with a loaded gun and the desire to kill? *Saving Sycamore* is the remarkable story of a woman whose compassion was stronger than the homicidal rage in the heart of a desperate student.

> —**Peter Langman, PhD**, author of *School Shooters: Understanding High School, College, and Adult Perpetrators*; director of Research and School Safety Training, Drift Net Securities

An incredible book written by an extraordinary human being. For some reason, Molly Hudgens was put in the position to lead a community through the unimaginable events at her school on September 28, 2016. *Saving Sycamore* illustrates Molly's leadership, compassion, faith, and vulnerability when the members of her school community needed her most on that fateful day and in the aftermath. This is a book about a faith journey.

> —**Frank DeAngelis**, principal of Columbine High School, 1996–2014; author of *They Call Me "Mr. De": The Story of Columbine's Heart, Resilience, and Recovery*

As a middle school counselor, I was awed by Molly's ability to put into words the battles we fight in our own hearts and minds as we try and navigate through the minefields and walls that so often surround the lives of young people. I would highly recommend this story for all to read as it gives to each of us the encouragement needed to face the fears and difficulties we encounter in life. It inspires each of us to reach out in love to those who are hurting.

> —**Gary Beikirch**, Medal of Honor recipient; author of *Blaze of Light*

The Citizen Honors award shows that the average person possesses the same characteristics that the Medal of Honor recipients are recognized for. Not on the field of battle but in everyday life. The Medal of Honor recipients believe everyone has those characteristics and only need the opportunity to take the actions to demonstrate them. Molly Hudgens stepped up and saved an individual and protected an entire school. This book and her story will stand as a guide for all educators to mediate tragedies in schools by identifying problems before they turn violent.

—Charles C. Hagemeister, Medal of Honor recipient

Full disclosure: I already knew this story as I have the honor of working with Molly Hudgens. Regardless, I could not put this riveting book down. This amazing story is masterfully woven into a tapestry of suspense and grace with God as the major thread. You will be beyond blessed in multiple ways as you read this compelling tale.

—Cathy Beck, director of Cheatham County Schools; author of *Mice in the Ivy* and *Leading Learning for ELL Students*

We want our young people to know they don't have to go into combat to become a hero. In conjunction with our Character Development Program (CDP), we honor citizens who are heroes and never went to war to become heroes. Molly is one of those we honored, and she is a perfect example of the citizens we hope to develop in our CDP. Her book will set an example and should be an inspiration to our educational community. I cannot recommend it too highly.

—Pat Brady, Medal of Honor recipient; author of *Dead Men Flying*

In *Saving Sycamore*, Molly Hudgens, through her words, but more importantly, through her actions on that September day, shows us that through faith, we can conquer anything, and often do the unthinkable. Molly was chosen to serve as an instrument of God, and her commitment to that immense responsibility saved the lives of many, and generations will be the recipients of her heroism and bravery. *Saving Sycamore* is an inspiring narrative that was cultivated from what was supposed to be another horrific tragedy. Faith and bold action won the day, and we all should be so bold.

—Travis Ellis, cofounder of the Shepherd's Men; Congressional Medal of Honor Citizen Honors Recipient

Molly beautifully tells the story of how God prepared her and allowed her to calmly work with a troubled teenager that led not only to saving the teenager's life but hers as well. It is inconceivable how many students' lives were saved by deescalating the crisis and disarming the young student. *Saving Sycamore* is a must-read to learn how God worked to truly save lives at Sycamore Middle School.

—Major General William B. Raines, Jr., USA (retired); Charles H. Coolidge National Medal of Honor Heritage Center Executive Board

Guided by an unshakable faith and a deep-seated passion for prevention, Molly Hudgens realized her purpose one ordinary school day. She saved a child and a school community the day danger and darkness walked through her office door. Through the courageous recounting of that day—and a lifetime of preparation—Molly reveals that there is hope and healing for all of us when we are willing to stand in the gap for another. The story of *Saving Sycamore* is the story of changing—and saving—lives through God's perfect love and one woman's perfect faith.

—Michele Gay, cofounder of Safe and Sound Schools; mother of Josephine Gay, killed in the tragedy at Sandy Hook Elementary School

The kind of courage Molly Hudgens is endowed with can only be acquired by having a deep faith in God, a quiet spirit, and an inordinate amount of common sense. This is the story of one unusual woman, acting alone, defusing a tragedy in the making, saving and changing lives in the process.

—Charlie Daniels, singer-songwriter; cofounder of the Journey Home Project; author of *Let's All Make the Day Count: The Everyday Wisdom of Charlie Daniels; Never Look at the Empty Seats: A Memoir; Ain't No Rag: Freedom, Family, and the Flag;* and *The Devil Went Down to Georgia*

Often we may not even recognize that we need help. Sometimes it is a friend or family member, someone close who can see that for us. Sometimes it is someone from outside our circle, even a stranger, who comes to our aid. Asking for help may be the most difficult thing we can ever do. This hero's story is one of the sanctity of human life and someone's faint cry for help among the raging static that fills our everyday lives. I challenge everyone to be as acutely attuned to the quiet sounds that could prevent a tragedy.

—**John Coolidge**, grandson of Medal of
Honor Recipient Charles H. Coolidge

Courage and faith. The end result could have been horrific if it had not been for Molly Hudgens. Never underestimate the power of prayer in a difficult and seemingly impossible situation. Her courage and ability to listen to God's still, small voice saved her life, the life of the would-be shooter, and the lives of many others that day at Sycamore Middle School.

—**Sammy L. Davis**, Medal of Honor recipient and author of
You Don't Lose 'Til You Quit Trying, and **Dixie Davis**, wife, mom,
grandmother, and author of *Endless Love and Second Chances*

Saving Sycamore

THE SCHOOL SHOOTING
THAT NEVER HAPPENED

MOLLY B. HUDGENS

Saving Sycamore: The School Shooting That Never Happened
© 2020 Molly B. Hudgens

This book is available at special discounts when purchased in quantity for educational purposes or as premiums, promotions, or fundraisers. For inquiries and details, contact the publisher at books@daveburgessconsulting.com.

Published by Dave Burgess Consulting, Inc.
San Diego, CA
DaveBurgessConsulting.com

Scripture quotations taken from The Holy Bible, New International Version® NIV® Copyright© 1973 1978 1984 2011 by Biblica, Inc. TM Used by permission. All rights reserved worldwide.

Library of Congress Control Number: 2020941031
Paperback ISBN: 978-1-951600-36-5
Ebook ISBN: 978-1-951600-37-2

Cover design and interior design by Liz Schreiter

Editing and production by Reading List Editorial: readinglisteditorial.com

This book is dedicated to my husband, Jason, and our two sons, Bradley Todd and Henry James. May you always know that you are my greatest gifts. Every day with you since September 28, 2016, has been a blessing of borrowed time.

To the 2016–2017 staff members of Sycamore Middle School: This is not my story; it is our story. Because of the school family you created and the role you played on September 28, 2016, all of us, and our students, are survivors.

Administrators: Lisa Young and Robyn Miller

Carolann Adcock	Adam Farley	Kristen Mundy
Carla Anderson	Pam Forbes	Carlton Odom
Katie Arnold	Brandy Ford	Kathryn Viola Penzo
Sherry Bagwell	Samantha Watts Fry	Katie Petrone
Angelia Bailey	Rachel Garrison	Michael Petrone
Judy Bailey	Tracy Gillingham	Lindsey Plewa
Lisa Ballew	SRO Chris Gilmore	Kyle Quillen
Lyndi Barnhill	Starr Hardin	Kristy Rhemann
Mandi Batson	Debbie Harlinger	Steven Sellars
Mallory Beecher	Glenn Harlinger	Matthew Shuff
Deborah Boshers	Stan Harrington	Aimee Shute
Jesse Buck	Lori Hawkins	Brittany Smiley
Cindy Calton	Lisa Hayes	Sarah Smith
Sheryl Carney	Cory Hesselbacher	Elizabeth Southards
David Casesa	Ralph Hughes	Kristen Stewart
Kelly Cook	Lindsay Jurek	Beth Stokes
Paige Cooper	Belinda Knight	Mark Stone
Gail Stone Costa	Jennifer Lamb	Paige Towle
Dale Daniel	Colin Logue	Aaron Turnington
Brooke Daugherty	Lucy Longworth	Petra Walls
Christy Davis	Billie McBride	Tracy Warren
Gail DeBusk	Jill McCain	Bethany Weeks
Sheena Edgin	Alex Mink	Connie Weeks
Sherrie Everett	Jennifer Morris	Jennifer Winters

Contents

Foreword
by Cara VanWinkle Adney

When Molly called me on September 28, 2016, I immediately knew something was wrong. There was a stillness in her voice I had never heard before. I remember her saying something bad had happened and that she wanted to be sure I heard about it from her and not on the news. She paused for a half second, but during that time a thousand scenarios ran through my mind before she would begin to tell me what had occurred at school earlier that day.

This conversation was far different than any conversation we'd ever had. Molly's stories had always been filled with detail (as you'll soon learn) and, for a girl from the South, when she was excited, they were extremely fast-paced. This wasn't the case on September 28.

On this day, her voice was calm and steady. She kept everything brief, but I could feel her fear, relief, and resolve from her home in Ashland City, Tennessee, to mine in Stillwater, Oklahoma. As she spoke, I sat in silence, trying to process what the previous hours had been like for her. There were no words to say—I could only listen and thank God that she had the faith and strength to connect with this young man and prevent something disastrous from happening at Sycamore Middle School.

More than twenty years have passed since I first met Molly. I was a freshman at Western Kentucky University, and she was a sophomore who lived across from me in Central Hall. It didn't take long for us to become friends. Molly was outgoing, friendly, and most of all, she was welcoming. She's always had a way of making people feel comfortable and safe. Her spirit and soul are inviting. Even back then, when you were with her you could let your guard down and be vulnerable.

Cara VanWinkle Adney (right) was my college roommate at Western Kentucky University and remains a dear friend.

We spent two years as neighbors before we became roommates during her senior year. In the two semesters we lived together, we solidified a friendship like neither of us had ever experienced. As adults, time and distance pulled us in different directions, but months before this fateful day, Molly and I had reconnected. Through our hundreds of text messages and countless phone calls, we discovered that in our time apart, both of us had taken up running. Now, Molly and I were *really lazy* in college, so the fact that we both now ran was quite a shock! Molly wanted to complete a full marathon and I wanted an excuse to return to Western. We decided that the bg26.2 race would be a perfect fit. She would run the full marathon, and I would run the half marathon and be there to celebrate her finish. When we committed to this event in early 2016, we had no idea how important this planned reunion would end up being.

It was no surprise when Molly told me she had moved from the classroom to school counseling. I instantly knew this was a perfect fit for her. In many ways, she'd been counseling people for years. During our dorm days, friends from our floor would frequently seek Molly's advice and guidance. She'd helped me through the loneliness of being an only child away from home for the first time, multiple breakups, nearly failing a class, changing college majors, and more. But I wasn't the only one who found comfort through her. You could rarely walk into Room 502 without seeing someone sitting on the edge of the raised twin bed, pouring out a problem or seeking Molly's input. I think this was partially due to her outgoing personality, but it was also the fact that we knew how important her faith was to her.

During college, when a lot of people question their faith and make questionable decisions after tasting freedom for the first time, Molly held fast to her values and beliefs. She would frequently return home to attend the Free Will Baptist Church she grew up in (which, for years because of her accent, I thought was the "For Real" Baptist Church) and she always kept a Bible near her bed. Her family has always been essential to her. I can still recall meeting her parents for the first time—David (Daddy) had on his denim overalls, and Shirley (Momma) had perfectly manicured hair and the warmest smile. Meeting them made it easy to see where Molly got her sense of humor and heartfelt compassion.

Looking back, it truly seems like Molly had been preparing throughout her entire life for the events of September 28, 2016. Attending a small Christian school allowed her to develop meaningful, personal relationships with her classmates and teachers. This experience shaped her commitment to really knowing her students in the classroom and the community. She moved out of state for college and had to learn to believe in herself—even when she was coming close to failing. This would help her connect with students who were struggling with their self-worth and what to do with their lives. Before graduating from Western, she found her dream guy and her dream job in her hometown.

This gave her a strong sense of belonging and community. A national tragedy piqued her interest and sent her love of learning, reading, and research into overdrive. This turned into an opportunity to teach a different type of student. And all of this prepared her for a student to walk into her office with a loaded gun.

Her actions on September 28, 2016, protected the lives of students at Sycamore Middle School. But the reality is, she has likely helped save more people than that. Through sharing her story, she has been able to connect with teachers, school counselors, law enforcement, and community members to remind them that they, too, have the power to be somebody's hero. Being a hero isn't as daunting or as overwhelming as it sounds. As Molly's story shows, some of the most important heroic elements are being present, aware, and willing. As you read this book, ask yourself who in your world is crying out to be saved. Once you know, follow Molly's lead and do your best to help them.

In the following story, you will read my version of the events of September 28, 2016. These remembrances are my own and are, to the best of my knowledge, the truth in regard to that day. Out of respect for this child and his privacy, I have chosen to omit his name and refer to him as "the young man," or "the student," rather than using a pseudonym, as it just never felt right to do so. This young man could have been anyone in any school or classroom in our country. It is my hope that the reader will envision a child in crisis they have known and come to believe as I do that every child is worthy of being saved— even from themselves.

Introduction

*N*ow they are seniors in high school . . . the eighth-grade class of 2016–2017. I have watched them leave middle school, spread their War Eagle wings at our neighboring high school, and learn to drive. They have participated in marching band competitions (winning state for three consecutive years), played many games on our fields and courts, and are preparing to take college entrance exams with their eyes on the horizon of their futures. They are all survivors. None of them was a victim or a fatality on September 28, 2016. At eighth-grade Class Day, I told them all that their being present for awards day—all of them—was my greatest blessing.

When I look back on that remarkable day in September, I am reminded that we are a miracle. Each one of us who was present on our campus that day—including the young man involved—is alive and able to chart a course for another day. We are not mourning, grieving, or attempting to cope with devastating loss and horrifying memories. We are intact, and our flag still flies at full staff.

School violence across our country has become far more commonplace than any of us can bear. Somewhere in the heartache and devastation of the loss of lives in our schools, we have come to believe that hope is lost and that one act of violence only precipitates another. Many have lost faith in the protection that our educational institutions provide, while others live in fear that an incident of violence will affect their own school or community.

Somewhere in this history of school violence, you find us: the school shooting that never happened. We are a campus that experienced a near tragedy, yet—driven by a group of dedicated educators—found a way to shield our students from long-term trauma. We were never perfect, but on that day, we were enough to protect, love, support, and shepherd our students to safety, including one who was struggling to save himself.

Every morning, I marvel at how much I still love that place. The smell of school supplies and preteen adrenaline combine with the sounds of laughter and learning. The transition between childhood and adulthood starts here, and as children begin to find themselves we are blessed to be part of the process. Sycamore is my second home and its staff a family—a family I love and hold dear. It is the only place I have ever worked as an educator, and it is my hope to stay here until my retirement.

I have been inspired by some of our nation's greatest educators who have endured tragedy and have remained there, in the face of it. From these great heroes, I have learned that a traumatic event need not force us to flee. In fact, we can stay, continue to thrive, and be effective in a school that holds great significance for us.

For me, seeing our former students succeeding in their career-driven classes, participating in service-oriented activities, and finding themselves as young adults is proof that God is good, and His plan for their lives continues. I cannot wait to see each of them fulfill their purpose and feel that maybe I had some small part in their future successes.

This story is theirs, mine, and ours—but above all, it is God's. He prepared me that day for the fight of my life and made me a warrior on my knees. It is to Him, and to all of our staff and students, that I am forever indebted. Any credit I have been given or glory I have received belongs to God and to them. We are Sycamore—the Knights—and on one unprecedented day in the history of school violence, we got it right.

Part I

The Preparation
and
the Protection

ᵗᵍ 1 ᵍᵗ

That Morning

Hindsight brings such insightful perspective: that Wednesday was just an ordinary day. It started with a ten-mile run. I was training to run the Bowling Green (bg26.2) marathon, and I ran 9.69 miles on the treadmill before it overheated. I completed the remainder of the last mile around the pool in our backyard. It was cool that morning, and the mist rising off the water's surface was a sure indicator that fall was in the air. My husband, Jason, had left for work before my run was over, so we missed each other. I would regret this later, but at the time I gave it very little thought.

It was Wednesday, September 28, 2016.

I remember getting dressed for work, pausing briefly in front of a full-length mirror in our bedroom, wondering if it was too late in the summer to wear a skirt with a black-and-white palm tree pattern. I decided the skirt would be fine. The kids wouldn't care what I wore, and it was comfortable. After studying my jewelry options, I decided to wear my favorite necklace—a thin silver plate with the words "I am enough" engraved on it in a mixture of cursive and print. How prophetic the necklace's simple words would prove to be shortly thereafter.

After rushing the kids out the door, I drove to Pleasant View, where I dropped our youngest son, Henry, at daycare before dropping Bradley, our oldest, off at his baseball coach's house. The coach's son was one of Bradley's best friends, and the opportunity to have breakfast, play some basketball, and delay his arrival at school by some thirty minutes was much more appealing than being dropped at the front door by Mom.

When I arrived at Sycamore Middle School, students were already milling around the flagpole. It was See You at the Pole day, when students across the country gather in a circle to have prayer at the base of their school's flag. I scanned the crowd, ensuring that there were sufficient parents and staff to supervise the students, and then hurried on to the school's entrance. I intended to put my things away and return to join the kids. These good intentions were short-lived.

Glenn Harlinger—my coworker in the school counseling department—and I were our school's Junior Beta Club sponsors. Our Junior Beta students are seventh and eighth graders with stellar academic records who perform service-oriented projects in our school and community. That Wednesday, as new Junior Beta inductees were arriving to the counseling department to turn in forms and fees, I busied myself directing students to Glenn's office while putting away my things and preparing for the day. I turned on my computer and was in the act of lighting a candle when a familiar student came in. Nothing about his appearance was cause for concern. It was a cool, fall Tennessee morning, and students had begun to wear jackets and hoodies for warmth. I smiled when we made eye contact, saying, "Hey, honey, what's going on?" I assumed he was coming to bring Junior Beta fees, but he wasn't.

He smiled and replied, "Would it be okay if I came to talk to you during Related Arts?"

I said that would be fine, as I didn't have any meetings scheduled during that time. Another exchange of smiles, and he left. There was never any hint of danger or foreboding. Ironically, I had just spoken to him for the first time the previous Friday for individual counseling, so I was slightly curious as to what he needed to discuss. But he was one

Glenn Harlinger, my counseling teammate, was my
ninth-grade algebra teacher and high school principal.
We worked together in the counseling department for
six years before his retirement in May 2020.

of our kids who needed to talk, and talking to kids was my favorite part
of my job.

I checked the water in the coffeemaker, filled the water pitcher, and
put the previous day's dishes away. As I grabbed a cup to fill with ice,
I remembered I left my tablet in our vehicle. I always listen to music
at school, so I reminded myself that I would need to run out later
to grab it out of the back seat. Little did I know I would never have
that opportunity.

I left my office and headed out on what Glenn and I called "our
rounds." We walked the hallways of our entire school each morning
in an effort to speak to students and teachers. These walks gave us the

opportunity to troubleshoot any problems that may have arisen prior to the start of the school day. Bad mornings, forgotten lunches, dress code issues, and running late are all factors that weigh heavily on kids and can cause a bad start to their day. Sometimes having an adult to assist in navigating these moments can help the day run more smoothly.

I don't remember any specific conversation I had that morning. A former student, Paige, was now our art teacher, and that Wednesday she was struggling with the late stages of pregnancy. We talked about that briefly, and then I headed down the fifth- and sixth-grade hallways before moving on to seventh and eighth grades. I love all of our students, but the upperclassmen are definitely my favorite. My worst year of school was seventh grade, and my best year was eighth grade. I also taught seventh and eighth grades prior to becoming one of the school counselors, so I feel a special connection with that age group.

It would seem eerie later to see myself on the school's surveillance video traversing the hallways. I stopped in the eighth-grade hallway to speak to three of our male faculty members—David, Dale, and Matthew. I had completed classroom guidance in Dale's and Matthew's classes the previous day, and we discussed that briefly. David and I have worked together for many years, and the surveillance footage would show that I straightened his twisted lanyard before heading back to my office. Then I checked the exterior doors—another ritual that, as part of our school's safety and crisis team, I performed every morning.

After returning to my office, I prepared breakfast and headed over to meet with Glenn to discuss our plans for the day. He was counting and logging Junior Beta money, and I commented on how glad I was to have a day back in my office after teaching the previous day. Glenn looked up to notice a student coming in his door. It was the child who had dropped in earlier that morning asking to speak with me.

He said, "Mrs. Hudgens, would it be okay if I met with you during RTI instead of Related Arts?" Response to Intervention was a remediation and enrichment class period. I realized that he must have felt he could not wait until later in the day for our discussion.

I said, "Sure, honey, head on over to my office. I'm going to gobble down these last few bites and I'll be right there." I forked down the rest of my breakfast, told Glenn I'd see him in a few minutes, and dropped my plate in the sink in the outer office, reminding myself to return and wash it later. I entered my office and saw the student was already seated in one of my chairs. I thanked him for waiting as I entered the room, and I closed the door behind me.

It was 8:07 a.m.

☙ 2 ❧

My Beginning

I was born on September 29, 1976, in Nashville, Tennessee, the only child of David and Shirley Bradley. My mother was a stay-at-home mom until I began the second grade, when she became the advertising and sales manager at our hometown newspaper, the *Ashland City Times*. My dad worked with my uncle Jimmy at the Bradley and Son Sawmill, which my grandfather started when they were boys. It sat right on the outskirts of Ashland City, Tennessee. Thinking about my childhood makes me smile. I was fortunate enough to grow up in a small town and live in the same house with both parents all of my life. With the exception of my aunt Dimple, who lived in Dothan, Alabama, until her passing in 2020, all of my parents' siblings live in Cheatham County.

I was born with a love for reading and books, and my parents thought I would be either a teacher or a doctor. I loved to play both. I started kindergarten at four years old and spent more than my fair share of time in the "sugar chair" for talking without permission. Many teachers during my elementary school years informed my parents that the only trouble I ever got into at school was for talking. I love to remind them today that I found a profession where I get paid to talk all day, and it's turned out just fine!

**As a child I often pretended to be a doctor or a teacher.
My parents felt certain I would be one
or the other. I still love reading to students.**

I loved school and was very rarely absent. I think I was afraid something exciting might happen and I might miss it! Although I struggled in math, reading and writing came easily to me. I was thrilled beyond words when my elementary school teacher allowed me to read aloud to our class during "rest time" each day. I practiced voices for the characters, working on inflection, because I didn't want my classmates to get bored. Those daily readings greatly influenced my later reading aloud to students in my own classroom. My greatest joy as a teacher came when, upon looking up from a book we were reading together as a class, I found the eyes of my students transfixed on me (and not the book) as I read to them . . . waiting to hear what would happen next.

Somewhere during those early elementary years, I decided I would become either a teacher or a school psychologist. People who worked in the field of school psychology helped kids solve problems, and I wanted to do that, too.

Being an only child forced me to use my imagination to entertain myself. My teachers made such an impact on my life (especially Mrs. Lawrence in first grade and Mrs. Trotter in fifth grade) that I spent countless hours playing school in my room. I would line up all my stuffed animals and dolls and instruct them, often hugging them to tell them how special they were. Those teachers along with my kindergarten teacher (my aunt, Barbara Jenkins) showed me how to love students by the way they respected, encouraged, and praised me.

My dad was the youngest son of nine siblings, falling into line at number eight. Due to the size of my extended family, I particularly enjoyed the holiday seasons, when I could play with my cousins. My closest cousin growing up was Stacey, the daughter of my mom's only sibling, my aunt Judy. Stacey was one year older and also an only child. We spent the summers together playing on our grandparents' farm, riding bikes, playing in the creek, and climbing in the forbidden hayloft of the barn to secretly create an amazing playhouse. We made mud pies, worked on science experiments, danced, and played with our Barbie dolls. I had a vivid imagination and Stacey was willing (on most occasions) to go along with my ideas.

Stacey's family lived a short distance from my grandparents, so sometimes after staying too late at Stacey's house I would ride my bike back to my grandparents' house in the twilight. The darkening sky mingled with the loud croaking of frogs and the deafening sound of summer insects made my ride back frightening.

I remember pumping my bike pedals as fast as I could, chanting, "When I am afraid, I will trust in Thee," over and over in my head. I rode all the way up to my grandparents' door, slammed on the brakes, and leaped from the bike to the sidewalk. My grandmother always told me I scared her to death when I came barreling in, out of breath and red faced from the exertion.

At the age of four, I began taking dance classes—ballet, tap, and jazz—and continued to do so until middle school, when I became a cheerleader for the Pleasant View Christian School Warriors. PVCS was an essential part of my childhood. Our class was small (I eventually graduated with only eleven other people), but we were part of a community of parents, grandparents, faculty, and staff who truly loved us and invested a great deal of time and effort to teach us morals and godly principles. We were our own small family and were sheltered from much of the world outside of our little community. We were healthy, happy, and well educated. The foundation of my faith was solidified there at Pleasant View Christian, and I still credit the men and women there for cultivating that faith.

Another driving force in the development of my faith was my paternal grandmother, Mabel Bradley. We all called her Grandmama, and though she was a petite lady, we all knew she meant business. She often took me to her church and gave me a dime for the offering plate on Sunday nights. She also introduced me to the Home Demonstration Club, where the older ladies took me under their wings and proved to be examples of graciousness and models of character.

Grandmama kept a box of missionary cards beside her bed, and on special weekends when I got to spend the night with her, she let me choose a missionary and their family from the box. After I selected a card, we knelt beside her bed and folded our hands on top of the mattress. Then, we prayed for that family. I would listen intently as Grandmama also prayed for our family, and especially for me. In a way I could never describe, I learned how much she loved me through her words to God. There were so many grandchildren, but Grandmama somehow made each of us feel special. After she passed away I continued to pray, but I am ashamed to say that very few times were on my knees. Later, on that fateful day in September at Sycamore Middle, when I was brought to my knees beside a hurting child, it was praying with my grandmother that I remembered.

At nine years old I made the decision to accept the faith of my family and asked Christ to come into my heart and save me. I remember kneeling on a little stool beside my bed and reading a prayer from a pamphlet I had received at school. That stool still sits beside my bed today as a constant reminder of that special night in my room, by myself, when I accepted God's promise of salvation.

My middle and high school years were filled with volleyball and cheerleading—and the usual angst that comes with being a teenager.

My parents, David and Shirley Bradley, have been a
constant in my life. They strongly supported my academic
and athletic endeavors at Pleasant View Christian School,
which provided much of the foundation for my faith,
and continue to remain two of my biggest fans.

Seventh and eighth grades were the hardest years of my life because
an allergic reaction caused white spots to appear on my legs. We never
learned what caused this allergy. Steroid shots intended to address the
allergy caused weight gain despite my involvement in extracurricular
activities. My self-esteem waned, and the person who had been my best
friend since second grade met a new friend and our friendship changed.
I felt alone, and I was devastated when I didn't place in a local beauty
contest at our county fair. The idea of ever being a princess was short-
lived after that loss.

Although I had loving parents who were very involved in my life,
I questioned if anybody loved me. My friends all seemed to have boy-
friends, and I entered into an unhealthy relationship with a boy who
made degrading comments to me. For reasons I now cannot comprehend, I stayed in that relationship for several months. When he ended

it, I was hurt and blamed myself. Suicide was never something I actively considered, but I did wonder if anyone would care if I was no longer around.

So many of the issues I faced during those two years resurface for me at work as I watch students face the same challenges. These situations seemed so overwhelming to me at the time, but today I am grateful for each one of them. When I sit with a girl who is experiencing the same hurt I did, I can honestly tell her I understand and help her to see years down the road.

Many times I have said, "Honey, you may feel as if you are in a valley right now and that you can't see anything in front of you except a mountain you must climb. The truth, however, is that I have seen the other side—and the view is going to be amazing. You will get there. All you need is time and the willingness to climb."

During the years of my middle school struggles, I began to spend time with my aunt Kathy, my dad's youngest sister. She had three sons who were all close to me in age, and her house was always full of her boys and their friends. I would ride along with Aunt Kathy and Uncle Buddy to watch the boys' baseball games, and Aunt Kathy taught me to keep stats. Probably because she wasn't my mother, I listened to her advice and began to see myself in a different light. Aunt Kathy wasn't afraid to say what she felt, but she was also one of the most observant people I had ever known and had an admirable insight into other people. From her, I learned to be assertive when necessary and honest when needed, but I also learned that building a relationship with a person is crucial toward having a true impact on them. She has remained a consistent pillar of support in my life, and I am so grateful for the influence she had on me during those difficult years.

By the end of eighth grade, my life was turning around! I made the varsity cheerleading squad, and after my date changed his mind just a few weeks shy of the super-important Valentine's Day Banquet at school, I was shocked when a popular upperclassman named Brad learned about the situation and offered to go with me to the banquet. I have never forgotten Brad's gesture of kindness. After the events of September 28, 2016, Brad—head of students at a private Christian school in Mississippi—left a moving post to me on Facebook. Over the months to come, I would be reunited with several childhood friends, and I would discover they were very much still family. There truly are no friends greater than your childhood friends.

The next year, as a ninth grader, I learned of a middle school boy who did not have a date for the Valentine's Banquet, and I decided to go with him. That became my first experience in paying it forward, and when he arrived at the banquet with a girl two years his senior, his friends were impressed. He and I would go on to become best friends (more like brother and sister, as he was an only child also) through high school. Back then, in the early nineties, we didn't have the technological advances we do today, and we slowly but surely lost contact. His friendship is one that I hope will return to me at some point, as some of my most cherished high school memories involve him and his family.

Our small school allowed us to be surrounded by a faculty and staff—as well as by a slew of families—who shared our faith and were truly invested in us. I now realize I had so much extended family, as the parents of my classmates played such a role in guiding my life. Mike and Brenda Mason were like second parents to me, and many of our school families influenced my life in such an impactful way. Rebecca Roberson, my high school science teacher, became arguably the most influential adult in my life. When I graduated, I planned to attend Western Kentucky University in Bowling Green, Kentucky, for the simple fact that Mrs. Roberson had also attended WKU. If it was good enough for her, then it was good enough for me. Mrs. Roberson and I stayed connected, and she is still one of my favorite people.

Another teacher with a huge impact on my life was Margaret Patton, my senior English teacher. Mrs. Patton also taught theater (or "drama," as we called it back then) and had a flair for reading and presenting. Each month, she asked our class to memorize a poem that we would recite for a grade. I kept every copy of those poems and, years later, when I would go on to teach my own eighth-grade language arts classes, I asked my students to memorize those same poems. "Hope" by Emily Dickinson, "A Bag of Tools" by R. L. Sharpe, "The Road Not Taken" by Robert Frost, "The Builder" (whose author is unknown), "If" by Rudyard Kipling, "New Beginnings" by Helen Steiner Rice, and "In Flanders Fields" by John McCrae—they were all great works I committed to memory and have used throughout my life for encouragement. Unbeknownst to Mrs. Patton or to me, those poems were, without a doubt, a prediction of my life to come.

I feel God has given me three gifts. The first one is my ability to talk to people: I never shy away from a conversation, and my parents will be the first to tell you that, even as a child, I never met a stranger I didn't like. People have always fascinated me—the way they all come from varied backgrounds and life experiences. Being an only child meant that I spent a lot of time in the company of adults, and on more than one occasion I was told that I had "an old soul."

The second gift is a talent for reading and an understanding of the written word. I was able to read before I started kindergarten at the age of four. Words came together for me, both on the page and in my mind, with ease. As a third grader, I discovered I could read upside down and backward. We would often read to younger children at school, and I noticed I could hold a children's book open in my lap facing the kids and read the text looking down at the page. I never thought it was an unusual ability, but I later found very few people were capable of performing that same task. Words, I realized, were just something I was meant to understand.

I devoured books and was delighted when my parents encouraged me to work at our public library during the summer between my seventh- and eighth-grade years. I loved mysteries, and I read all of the Nancy Drew series that summer. I developed a habit I've continued long into adulthood: reading the last chapter of every mystery novel first. I want to know who the killer is so I can watch that character throughout the book. It's never a matter of suspense for me; I just want to understand the characters' actions and motives. This habit doesn't ruin the story for me; rather, it enhances it.

As an adult I became drawn to stories of true crime, crises, and tragedy, but I also sought out biographies and autobiographies about people who overcame great odds to survive amazing challenges. I never knew why those topics interested me, never particularly noticed my choice of books until after September 28.

In the weeks leading up to the incident at Sycamore, however, I was reading three books: *Fighting Back* by Deena Burnett, the wife of a passenger on Flight 93, which crashed in Pennsylvania on September 11, 2001, after Tom Burnett and the other passengers made a valiant effort to take back control of their hijacked airliner; *Highest Duty: My Search for What Really Matters* by Chesley "Sully" Sullenberger, who successfully landed a crippled airplane in the Hudson River in 2009 without losing the life of even one passenger; and *A Mother's Reckoning: Living in the Aftermath of Tragedy* by Sue Klebold, whose son was one of the school shooters at Columbine High School in Colorado in 1999. Unbeknownst to me, I was being prepared for my own battle, and many of the heroes I encountered in past books and stories directly affected my thought processes and actions that day.

The third gift I was granted is a passion and drive for completing whatever task has been set before me. It was very difficult for me to keep my highly competitive nature in check, even in my early years of school. I worked to achieve a trophy every year for Bible memorization, and I enjoyed reading more books than my classmates. My true competitive spirit would not emerge until high school, when I became fully involved in sports.

For people who do not consider cheerleading a sport, you have never picked up someone who weighs 100-plus pounds and hoisted them over your head for several minutes, or thrown them up into the air before catching them in a perfect "cradle" at the end of their descent. The physical part of cheerleading is only half of it. Cheerleading is really about morale boosting and being optimistic even when your team is losing by twenty points. But the hidden lesson that cheerleading provides is one of leadership, showmanship, and teamwork.

Cheerleading today is a highly competitive sport in which students compete to land the perfect tumbling pass, hit every mark in a choreographed routine, and score points for delivering difficult stunts and engaging the crowd. I spent middle and high school as a cheerleader, and I loved it. We had the best seats in the house, and as someone who loved sports, I was able to see amazing shots and carefully orchestrated plays from the sidelines. Being part of my school's athletic scene connected me to friends and classmates in a way that another role could never have provided.

I also played volleyball, as did almost everyone on our cheerleading squad. In fact, very few people gave the cheerleaders a hard time about not being athletes because all of us played at least one other sport. In volleyball I was a server, a setter, and a sitter. I was good at serving, but a girl one year younger than me was excellent. Our nickname for Tracie on the team was Quince because she was known on many occasions to serve fifteen straight points.

I played the position beside Tracie in the back court, so she and I developed a fun game of "calling" serves. I would hold up a number of fingers, and she would attempt to serve to that area of the court. Actually, I am fairly certain I had no idea which position I was calling—so she probably just served it where she wanted to—but I learned our little scheme had a psychological effect on the other team—as did a little pregame warm-up we performed. Our team would storm into the gym, run the perimeter much as a basketball team does, and then break into two-man teams to practice "bumping"—volleyball language at the time for warming up. We performed this little pregame exhibition very seriously, and never smiled. I noted that some teams would even stop and watch us, showing me that confidence, when channeled accurately, could be extremely effective. Even if you don't feel confident, sometimes it only matters that you *appear* to be so.

I would remain competitive throughout my life, although not always athletically. I still enjoyed the rush of adrenaline and the feeling of euphoria achieved through completing a task or engaging a class. It was important to me to perform well and to know that others recognized my effort and the results it produced.

❧ 3 ❧

The First Ten Minutes

Upon entering my office, I noticed the young man was already seated in one of my brown student chairs with his back to me. He didn't turn to face me as I approached, which I later realized was another initial indicator that something was amiss. Almost every student who awaits me acknowledges my arrival—but he did not. I walked around him and seated myself in my desk chair. It was a fairly warm morning, but the student was wearing a gray jacket zipped all the way up to his chin. This was not too unusual—many teenagers, unsure of their changing bodies, seek comfort in oversized sweatshirts and layers of clothing—but there was something about the way it was zipped all the way up that reminded me of our youngest son. Henry had just learned to zip himself into his own jacket and would run the zipper all the way to the top just for good measure.

The student seemed slightly agitated, but that, again, was not unusual. Most kids are hesitant to divulge problems or challenges they are facing. They are adolescents, and much of middle school is awkward or uncomfortable in some way. I reached for the pair of magnets I keep attached to the inside of my desk. I often play with them while talking with students, pulling the magnets apart and then allowing them to spring back together. Having something in my hands while talking helps me focus. Fortunately, students very seldom comment on them or even notice them, as I keep them discreetly in my lap. I'm not sure when that habit first evolved, but after eleven years it has become second nature.

It's funny how the mind processes traumatic events. Many times it will take a person months or even years to remember the specifics of the event in question. Sometimes they never remember all of it and must rely on other witnesses to fill in the gaps. Here, there were no witnesses. The young man and I have only seen each other one time since that day in September, and we didn't speak of those events at that time. I hope that someday, when time has passed, he will be able to come forward and tell his own story: I believe it would be a powerful example of how people still have a choice to control their futures, even when standing on the edge of a precipice considering something that would change the lives of so many in a terrible way. Until that day comes, however, the events that follow are from my memories alone, and they are as accurate as I know them to be.

Today I remember his face, but for many months afterward, I could not.

That morning I focused on his eyes, as I always do, attempting to show students that I am present and truly listening. He struggled to make eye contact, and his eyes darted furtively around the room. I glanced around myself in an effort to see what was distracting him, but I saw nothing. I again focused on his face, making an effort to understand what he was having difficulty saying.

Kids do not always have words readily available to them. Some of counseling requires waiting patiently for students to find the words so they can explain—to the best of their abilities—what is concerning them. This can be difficult and sometimes the quiet lapses can be frustrating for adults, but I always attempt to give students time to find their own words and present their situation as best they can from their perspectives. The truth is relative in these situations. What really matters is their perception.

While the student was visibly agitated, finding it difficult to maintain eye contact, he also made it clear to me that he was upset about something with his fidgeting and unease. I started the conversation as I have so many other times with hundreds of students: I said, "So, babe, what's going on?" It took him a few moments to verbalize anything at all. He kept putting his hands into his outer coat pockets and taking them out again. During this silence, I noticed my heart rate increase. I knew immediately this surge in adrenaline was an indicator that something was not as it should be. I believe we all have a gut instinct, something primal inside us that warns us of danger. I noted the change in my own body, wondered momentarily if it meant something, and refocused.

I have chosen not to include any exact dialogue here or in the chapters to follow except for the phrases disclosed in the press conference by our county sheriff. This decision comes out of a respect for this child and my belief that it is his right to share his own words from that day at a time in the future if he so chooses. If he does not, then I will respect that decision and keep them always locked away inside myself. Some things are just meant to be kept sacred.

It became evident from what he shared that he had several issues going on in his life, each of which—in and of itself—did not appear to be a heavy burden. The combination of these issues, however, had swirled into a perfect storm. Weighed down by all of this, this student had come to me for help. As he began speaking in an agitated fashion regarding these issues, the young man unzipped his jacket and reached across his body into an inner pocket. Then, he began tapping on something.

Instantly, the blood began pounding in my ears. I had two thoughts: (1) He's right-handed, and (2) he has something in that pocket.

The room became eerily silent as I fought the urge to flee. Every synapse was firing in my brain.

Before he mentioned it, before he even said a word—I knew.

He had a gun.

Having spent many days evaluating that September morning, I cannot recall how I knew that this student was in possession of a firearm. I simply don't know. I believe God was preparing me, buying me minutes of time to formulate a plan for what would become the best-played mental chess match of my life.

When I was struck with the realization that a gun was most likely present, I remember feeling a warm sensation spread across the top of my head. It felt almost as if someone had poured a warm liquid on the crown of my head. The sensation made it feel as if it were trickling down the sides of my face and the back of my neck. My heart rate increased, and I remember noticing that I felt lightheaded. It was then that I experienced the first of many strong, internal directives that would drive the moments ahead. This directive would force me to refocus. *You're not going to faint.*

Could he hear my heart pounding in my chest? Everything inside of me wanted to scream for help or make a dash to the door. I frantically wished I could lock the young man in the room, but that wasn't possible: fire codes don't permit a locking mechanism of this type. Silently, without moving, I dismissed every option just as quickly as it had arisen.

I was trapped in a room with only one exit, directly behind the student. If he thought I was fleeing or trying to get help, then he would have no option. It would register in his young mind as a power struggle, with me attempting to gain the upper hand. The words *He'll shoot you in the back* flashed through my brain. I realized this was not a fight-or-flight situation. What was the best course of action? There seemed to be no good options.

You are their only protection. More thoughts, more words forced me to refocus. Directly across the hallway from our outer office, two classrooms of students were fully engaged in a lesson taught by my friends, Aaron and Kathryn. I thought about Aaron's three-year-old son and the fact that both classrooms were set up with the teachers' backs to the doors. I noted that classes would end in ten minutes as I stared at the clock on the wall behind the student. At that point, almost two hundred students would flood the hallway for a restroom and locker break. That routine would last approximately seven minutes.

I had to keep him talking. The look on his face was almost a smirk. I fought down rising panic.

It's the day before my fortieth birthday, and I'm going to die in my school wearing this skirt. This will be my crime scene photo. If I'd known I was going to die today, I'd have worn something different. That thought actually crossed my mind . . . along with the thought that my boys were going to grow up without a mother. *Did I teach them enough? Prepare them enough?* Tears clouded my eyes as I fought to swallow the sob that was building.

You will not cry. This thought blanketed me with an extreme calm, one I hoped to mirror in my demeanor. I breathed, and I listened as the young man talked about his trials. It was crucial to keep him engaged in conversation. Then, right outside my door, the kids began moving through the hallway. Panic rose again as I thought about how vulnerable they were. They seemed so loud and I worried their laughter, the slamming of locker doors, and the flushing of toilets in the girls' restroom adjacent to my back wall might interrupt his train of thought and draw attention to the proximity of potential victims.

I heard the door to our outer office open, and I prayed, *Don't come in here.* Teachers always dash in to grab beverages from the refrigerator or refill their coffee mugs—but now if even one of them attempted to enter my office, the entire setting would be disrupted and might serve as a catalyst for him to take action. I thanked God for the closed door, and I hoped teachers would interpret the closure as a request for privacy.

Meanwhile, the young man kept talking, and I fought to control my breathing as I strained to focus on his words.

It was during these moments that I first noticed it. Something was rising up inside of me . . . my pulse pounding in my ears, my fingertips almost numb. It would take months before I understood that it was a protective agent that would shroud me during the time to follow. A Medal of Honor recipient said it best when he proclaimed that "fear is not a weakness. Fear is a tool." God was preparing me for a fight. Fear combined with anger produces a protective agent that is difficult to describe in words. It is somewhat of a metaphorical armor for the mind that allows a state of laser-like focus. Time begins to move in slow motion, words are more distinct, and other senses seem to be indescribably enhanced.

Now, the thoughts—directives—became more succinct and vivid. *You are stronger than you've ever been. You have been prepared for such a time as this.* I had spent ten years studying and researching school shootings with a specific focus on the psychology of the shooters. Suddenly I understood why. As the young man talked on, I noticed the sounds in the hallway were growing dimmer. The kids were almost back in class. A sense of relief overpowered a sense of anger. *Not my school.* I remember locking eyes with him for a second in which I thought, *You're not leaving this room.* I knew what that might mean. *You'll have to kill me first, and I'm not going to make that easy.* I had never in my entire life thought about harming a child, but in those moments I knew I would do so before I allowed him to kill me or attempt to flee with the intention of harming students. Surprisingly, it was an easy decision.

Noting the silence in the hallway, I relaxed slightly. The students were back in class. Three doors now existed between them and the battle that was quietly raging in this young man's mind. I recall thinking, *No one in the world has any idea that this is going on right now except for me.* Meanwhile, he kept tapping on the object in his pocket. *You'll have to take the bait* was my next thought. Anger again welled up inside me. *Fine, I'll bite,* I thought. For some reason, this infuriated me—that I had to play along with this game. But he had to feel as if he had all of the power. I had to play a subservient role, despite how angry it made me.

I might have to ask him the question he wanted, but I would do so with a sarcastic slant. It was my one small form of rebellion. I'm sure my wording may have been nicer, but I thought, *So, what are you tapping on, Little Drummer Boy?*

༄ 4 ༄

Angels Unawares

ollege, for me, was akin to culture shock. Never in my wildest dreams would I have imagined that people didn't go to bed at ten o'clock on a "school night," that they'd skip classes, and some might never actually study. It was the first time I had lived outside of my comfort zone and also the moment I began to realize that not everyone had been as fortunate as I. So many people I encountered were struggling financially, emotionally, and spiritually. Our room was often filled with friends. Looking back, I believe that it was because—while I may have been shocked by some of the people I met and the choices they were making—I tried not to judge them. It was important for me to understand their situations.

That first semester I met a young man who had lost his dad and many friends in a horrific church bus crash in Carroll County, Kentucky, when he was in middle school. This friend was the first person I'd ever met who had endured devastating loss in such a public way. I purchased a book about the bus crash because he was my friend, and I wanted so much to understand his loss. He left after his first year to pursue his education at a different school, and we lost touch. I often think of him and his family and credit him for inadvertently teaching me about empathy on a different level.

That semester offered me another experience that foreshadowed that future September morning. College algebra was, simply put, not my forte. Our professor taught from a book she wrote herself, and this intimidated me. Despite my best efforts and never missing even one class, I could not grasp the concepts and perform well on tests. My parents hired a tutor, but still I struggled. I scored a 45 on my first test and was devastated about that number written in bold, red ink at the top of the page.

I gathered my belongings and headed to my next class, Health 100, in a building across the road. That class would not start for another hour, and I fought back tears as I climbed the stairs to the third floor and sank down in the hallway outside of the classroom door. Drawing my knees to my chest, I sobbed quietly with my head buried in my arms. I had graduated third in my senior class, and I was failing a college course. How could this be happening?

My biology class proved to be just as difficult, and now I felt doubly defeated. I made a decision to call my parents and admit that I needed to come home. Apparently I was not as intelligent as I thought myself to be. As I cried in the hallway, I remember praying, *Lord, I felt so strongly that You wanted me to come to school here . . . that You wanted me to become a teacher. What is happening? What am I supposed to do? Lord, please help me.*

Despite my labored breathing from crying, I became aware of someone moving down the hallway. Instantly, I wished I could disappear. Whoever the person was, he or she was bound to have heard me crying, and I was embarrassed. *Just please let them pass by*, I thought. But, of course, that was not to be the case. My face stained with tears, I looked up at the person standing, looking down at me. It was a guy—another student—who lowered himself to the floor and sat beside me.

"Hey, uh, are you okay?" he asked.

I remember trying to compose myself and telling him I was fine, that I had just not done as well on a test as I would have liked. He took the paper that was lying beside me on the floor and turned it over to reveal the grade.

"Ah, algebra, huh?"

I nodded, and he proceeded to share with me that freshman year was always the most difficult. His sympathetic tone and sincere attempt to encourage me were uplifting, and I found myself telling him my plight. I was attending college on a scholarship, and if I was unable to maintain a certain grade point average, I risked losing it. As my story poured out, that of a small-town girl from a tiny private school who had gone from being a big fish in a small pond to a little minnow in the huge ocean, he listened, nodding at intervals.

When I finished, he consoled me, patted my arm, and said, "Molly, everything is going to work out, and you're going to be just fine." I thanked him for listening as he rose from the floor, waved, and dismissed himself by telling me that he had to get to class and to "take care." Still embarrassed, I watched him as he walked away—just a regular guy dressed in jeans and a plaid shirt—and I wondered what he thought of me.

I bet he wishes he hadn't even stopped. I kicked myself for being so vulnerable, pouring out my heart to a perfect stranger. I considered skipping Health but decided to at least finish the class and the day before heading back to the dorm. Just before class began, I slipped off to the restroom to survey the damage to my makeup, wiped my tear-stained cheeks, and stared deep into my own eyes in the mirror. I had never quit anything in my life, and I was seriously considering whether or not to end my college career.

I decided to wait until the following day to tell my parents. The idea of disappointing them was devastating to me. That night, as I quietly mulled over the conversation with the guy in the hallway, I replayed some of the words he had said to me. Lying there silently under my quilt in the dark, I wondered if he could possibly be right. Would it get better? Could it possibly? It was there in the stillness with my roommate sleeping across the room that I prayed one more prayer of resignation before I drifted off to sleep.

My rest was fitful, and I tossed and turned dreaming of the student in the hallway. In the dream I could not see his face because my vision was so blurred from my tear-filled eyes. I remembered him leaning over and patting me on the arm.

Molly, everything is going to work out, and you're going to be just fine. In the dream my name reverberated off the walls. Unlike in real life, he repeated it over and over. Suddenly, I sat bolt upright in bed—wide awake. My heart pounded as I rummaged in a drawer for a flashlight I kept there. Trying not to wake my roommate, I fumbled through my backpack and pulled out the crumpled test. There it was: the 45 in bold, red ink, and beside it were four numbers—the last four digits of my social security number—a practice our teacher used so papers could be returned anonymously.

My hand clasped my mouth to stifle a sob, I unbolted the door, and I ran down the hallway to our community bathroom, where I locked myself in the last stall. I sobbed openly. Over and over I replayed the conversation, trying to make sense of it all. No matter how hard I tried, I could not remember his face. Sinking to sit on the toilet seat, I was forced to admit that at no time during our conversation had I ever told him my name—but somehow, some way, he knew. It wasn't on my test paper or my backpack or my clothing. This stranger, whose name I did not know and whose face I could not remember, knew my name.

The next day, I searched every binder and notebook . . . my name was on none of them. I waited outside my health class for a guy who would never appear. It would be weeks later, after many attempts at finding him by stalking the third floor, that I had to admit he did not exist. It was as if he had vanished. I began to think that maybe it had been some sort of delusion. Maybe I had dozed off in the hallway and had just dreamed it all? There was simply no good explanation.

It would be weeks later, when I was absentmindedly flipping through a devotion book that an older couple at our church had given me, that I stumbled upon the answer. I was looking for something on encouragement—still attempting to decide whether or not to even complete the semester—when I found it. The words leaped off the page and tears stung my eyes as I read: "Be not forgetful to entertain strangers: for thereby some have entertained angels unawares" (Hebrews 13:2 KJV).

I read the verse over and over again, straining my memory for some recognition of his face. I knew he was male. He was dressed like a college student. The hallway had been almost empty. It was September, and the temperature outside was still worthy of shorts and T-shirts, yet he had been dressed more warmly in flannel and denim. There were no wings. No halo. I shook my head, struggling to wrap my mind around this being. Could it be that in a moment when I was asking God for help He would send an angel in human form to comfort me? Was that even possible?

If that being had been supernatural—sent from God—then surely his words would have been prophetic. I knew no one would ever believe me, but I shared the story with a few relatives, including one of my aunts, who told me, "Faith is about believing in something you don't see or even understand, but that you know in your heart to be true." She went on to tell me, "Who are you to question? Why not just accept?" Relieved she didn't think I was crazy, I decided angel or not, that moment would be a turning point.

The first semester of my first year at Western had some shining moments. I met Tracey Kelley, a brown-haired girl from White House, Tennessee, who had grown up on a dairy farm. Tracey was the mother figure of our floor of the dorm and became a sounding board before eventually becoming one of my very best friends. If it had not been for Tracey's friendship and my underlying belief that God still wanted me to become a teacher, I probably would not have returned for my second semester of college.

I would continue to struggle in math, eventually failing the course. My biology class and my lab class grades were pretty dismal, too. But my saving grace came through my English classes. Despite only ever missing one class, the semester would end with my grade point average failing to even reach a 2.0, but my scholarship allowed a grace period of one semester to improve my average.

My faculty mentor reviewed my performance with me and graciously said, "Molly, if you want to teach, why not teach English? I mean, you made an A in that class." I was embarrassed by the obvious nature of his insight. Why was I determined to teach science when English was obviously my best subject? Over Christmas break, I would gather my pride, regroup, and set my sights on the next semester. As I drove home for the holidays, Amy Grant's "Tender Tennessee Christmas" played on

Tracey Kelley Bertram has been one of my dearest friends
since we met on the fifth floor of Central Hall on the
campus of Western Kentucky University in 1994.

the radio, and I remembered my divine intervention. I purposed in my heart to continue my education, and Hebrews 13:2 would become my life verse.

I decided getting a work-study job on campus might help me manage my time in a better fashion, so I applied for and was offered the job of secretary for the Industrial Technology department. It was there I found a host of professors and staff who offered support in the form of a work family. The administrative assistant became like a mom away from home. When we weren't sorting mail, making copies, answering the phone, directing students, or typing tests, we talked. Mrs. Judy was a great listener and such a supporter of me. My new desk job gave me access to a computer, so I was able to type papers and study when I wasn't busy.

During that second semester I found my footing, after altering my schedule to include more English and literature classes, along with volleyball. After final exams I nearly ran down the hill to climb into my already loaded car, and, after securing my pet fish, Pasqualli, and his bowl in my laundry bag, I headed home. When my grading report arrived a few weeks later, I had As in all of my English classes and volleyball. I can't say the same for math.

As sophomore year approached, my roommate and I settled back in to the same dorm room we had the previous year, and we held our breath as a new crew of freshmen arrived. It was during the following weeks that I met Cara VanWinkle. I wish there were words to describe her accurately, but even after twenty years . . . there just are not! Cara, like me, was an only child, and we quickly established an easygoing friendship. With her quick wit and self-deprecating personality, Cara and I enjoyed easy banter and deep conversations. Cara was a writer and found her niche working for the *College Heights Herald*. Although we were friends for the next two years, it wasn't until my senior year that Cara and I would become roommates and lifelong friends.

When I think back to my second year at WKU, I remember English classes, reading so much that I had to get glasses (I'd previously had twenty-twenty vision!), and working on papers. Endless papers. Aunt Judy and Uncle Jimmy had given me a word processor for high school graduation, so I was able to work in my dorm room rather than go to the library to wait in line for a computer—it makes me laugh now, seeing how accessible technology has become and how much Internet usage has grown.

During my second year of college my beloved grandmother, Mabel Bradley, passed away of a heart attack. We gathered at the hospital thinking she was just having heart palpitations only to learn that she had coded in the ambulance. Our laughter and talking faded to sorrow and tears as we realized she was gone.

For reasons I cannot remember, I was allowed to see her at the hospital. Her palm was still warm as I held her hand. I remember not being afraid at all, just wishing that I could see her spirit soar and have a small vision of what she was witnessing. I imagined a reunion with my grandfather and so many other family members, and I had a new understanding of grief that I still hold to today. We do not grieve for the loss of the loved one from our lives. We grieve because we could not go with them. We were created in Heaven, and all of us yearn to one day return there. I thought of Ecclesiastes: "A time to be born, and a time to die" (3:2 KJV).

For two days I prayed that she would come to me in a dream. I just wanted to be certain that the faith instilled in me and the belief of a life beyond this one was true. The night before her funeral, I was granted that request. There is very little I remember about the dream other than that she was present exactly as I knew her. It was so real that I could smell her perfume. I was home with my parents, and I got out of bed and began to write.

In the early hours of the morning I wrote a poem about my grandmama, and the next day I read that poem at her funeral. It was the first time I spoke before a public audience. I remember the faces of my family members and my dad bowing his head so I wouldn't see his tears. Any nervous energy and trepidation fell away as I tried to describe for all of us how very much we loved her. Since her death, I have thought of her and missed her many times. Her picture still sits atop our refrigerator in the kitchen, and I like to think that she is watching over me. I would feel her presence three other times in my life: my wedding day, one night when I held our sick baby son all night, and in my office on my knees on September 28. Oh, how very much I miss her and how grateful I am that she was there during the most terrifying ordeal of my life.

After college, I would share the story of the angel in the hallway as part of my testimony for a ladies' group in my church. I will never forget watching them nod in understanding and embrace my story. I was so overcome with emotion that anyone believed me. I had been afraid that they would think I had created the entire event. One of them hugged me afterward and listened as I explained my hesitation of sharing my story out of fear that it was just too unexplainable for others to believe.

As I pulled back to look at the lady, she said, "Oh, Molly, it was real. You can rest assured that any time you ask for God's help, He will respond in some way. You had only to believe that He would answer your prayer, and He did." Little did I know that almost twenty-two years

My paternal grandmother, Mabel Bradley, was my greatest faith influence. I remembered her in my office on September 28, 2016, as I prayed with a struggling child. She will be the first person I find when I reach Heaven's shores.

later, He would deliver again, and I would again be in the presence of an angel . . . on my knees . . . in a public school . . . on Holy Ground.

My perspective on safety changed in a mighty way my junior year in college, when my class was interrupted by two law enforcement officers who asked my professor if they could please see "Molly Bradley." I was terrified as they escorted me from the building, and I racked my brain as to what I could possibly have done that would require police intervention.

When they opened the back door of the police cruiser and allowed me to climb in, I realized I was not being arrested. The officers drove me down the tree-lined hill back to my dorm and opened the glass partition between the front and back seats to ask me a series of alarming questions: Had there been a relationship that had ended badly? Was I afraid of anyone? Had anyone been following me, contacting me, threatening me?

I finally suggested that if the officers could simply explain what was going on, I might be able to provide more insight. They explained that someone had contacted the state department of police in Kentucky to report that they had placed a bomb in Room 502 of Central Hall on the campus of Western Kentucky University. That was my room.

In the hours that followed, my roommate and I would go through our dorm room with agents from the Kentucky Bureau of Investigation. Anything that seemed out of place was cause for concern. After a thorough search, nothing was discovered. That night we lay awake listening for any strange sound, and I wanted more than anything to just go home.

Even now, no one knows who the culprit was or why they chose that specific room. One campus officer told me that, at the time, the number 502 was the police code for a bomb in Kentucky. I believe the caller chose that number with no connection at all to us. That situation, however, changed me.

Already a cautious person, I began to take even more notice of my surroundings. I never left campus alone and began reading about self-protection. I remember in particular one book called *Be Alert, Be Aware, Have a Plan: The Complete Guide to Personal Security* by Neal Rawls and Sue Kovach, which chronicled various scenarios involving danger and challenged the reader to imagine how they would react in the event that one of the scenarios actually occurred.

It was the bomb-threat situation that began my interest in crisis management, but it was the following year when I took a class called Marriage and Family that altered the course of my planned career. Our professor would encourage us to role-play a counselor/client scenario in class, and this is what first brought my awareness to the field of counseling.

That year our campus was taken by surprise when tornadoes mixed with hail swept through and damaged the area, including my car. As the car had been paid off, we signed a waiver with the insurance company never to report hail damage again on that car, and I decided to keep driving it, dents and all. The insurance settlement would allow me to go to graduate school for counseling. I was at the end of the Marriage and Family class, so I talked with my professor about the process for applying. After taking the GRE, I was accepted into the Mental Health Counseling program at Western. I continued to drive that dented car until 2005, although many people asked why I didn't trade it in for a new one. It served its purpose, and even today, I have only owned one other car since then. Maybe one day we'll buy another new one, but for now, I'm averaging one every fifteen years!

During my second semester of graduate school, a professor of adolescent psychology suggested I consider becoming a school counselor. He smiled when I informed him that my school had never had one, and I had no idea what they did. The explanation that followed led me to believe this might be the career for me. So, with little further persuasion, I changed my major to school counseling. It was, without a doubt, one of the best decisions of my life.

> *Have I not commanded you? Be strong and courageous. Do not be afraid; do not be discouraged, for the LORD your God will be with you wherever you go.*
>
> Joshua 1:9

❧ 5 ❦

The Gun

So, what are you tapping on, Little Drummer Boy?

I remember the look on his face, the power he exhibited knowing he felt in control over the situation. Rage encompassed me as my heart rate accelerated, growing loud enough that the pounding in my ears seemed to drown out all other sound. Almost.

He responded by telling me it was a pencil box on which he had been tapping. Of course it wasn't a pencil box. What eighth-grade boy carries a pencil box? None. I knew what the young man had inside his jacket, and I surmised that he was aware of that fact. He was playing a game, attempting to impress me and remind me of the power he possessed nestled in the lining of his coat. I glanced at the picture of my family on my desk. Jason and my boys. The thought that instantly followed was, *No . . . refocus. This is not about them.*

He began asking a series of questions that made my blood run cold. Each question was composed of a scenario, and he expected me to answer him by saying how I would respond if he took that specific course of action. My body was on red alert, such that I could see my eyelashes each time I blinked. I answered every question he presented with a question of my own. I could feel God supplying me with questions, as the words left my mouth faster than thoughts could formulate in my head. I knew that in some ways, it was already too late. The young man knew he had already gone too far. He indicated that he had done something bad, and that no one could help him. He told me he knew I was a good person but that he was not a good person. As heartbreaking as it was, it was even more devastating when he told me he felt as if he had met me too late. He said there were some issues that he needed to talk to someone about a long time ago. I was terrified that the pendulum had already swung too far in the wrong direction.

I assured him that we could work through anything he had done. Meanwhile, the entire time this conversation was taking place, my mind was racing. Should I try to contact someone? If so, who? How? As quickly as that thought came, an answer resounded in my mind: *No, you can't violate the trust you've established with him; then he'll have no choice but to kill you.* After studying the law enforcement investigations into school shootings for many years, I also knew that a child with a loaded gun and a potential hostage would automatically dispatch a SWAT team. During an officer training several years prior, I had witnessed police officers storming a classroom and opening fire. The trajectory of bullets in this small space could easily result in a fatality—which might be me. Then the phrase came to me: *No shots fired, no lives lost. You're going to have to talk your way out of this.*

I realized I was reading and rereading the words on my daily calendar: "You know you're a runner if . . . " Nothing in the text of the calendar page was of any help, but I found a calmness reading the bullet points numbering one to ten. He watched the candle flickering on my desk, and I thought about how it was against fire codes for me to have the candle. Suddenly the scent became overwhelming, and I covered the flame with the candle lid, leaving the smoke to swirl around within the glass dome.

He wanted to know what I was required by law to report to another entity. I ticked off the items that a counselor is required to report—abuse, potential crime, actual crime committed, suicidal threats—all in simple words. He seemed irritated by this list and began sweating profusely as he mulled them over. And then he said he had something to tell me. He was certain it would be something that I had never heard before.

I said, "Well, I've been doing this job for a long time. There's not many things that I haven't heard." But I knew. Deep down, I knew exactly what he was going to tell me.

He said, "I bet you've never had a student tell you he had a loaded gun before."

Nerves in my shoulders began to tingle, and without missing a beat, I responded, "Well, no, they haven't told me that, but you probably wouldn't be the first person to have brought one to school." Again, a sentence was leaving my mouth with absolutely no forethought, though my body elevated to another level of high alert.

Reaching inside his coat, the young man withdrew the weapon. As his hand extended from the fold of his jacket, I thought, *This is what happens when people die unexpectedly. They leave for work never knowing it will be the last day of their lives.* The gun was black, a semiautomatic weapon. The base of the firearm faced away from me, so I couldn't tell if there was a magazine inside, but a word was written on it. Reading—upside down and backward—I read "Millennium." I didn't recognize it. My first thought was that it was a Beretta—a 9mm—a weapon with which I was familiar, because we owned one.

Reaching into his outside pocket, the young man now produced a fully loaded magazine and a clip holder that would allow the magazine to be attached to his ankle. Without any thought or hesitancy, I stood up slightly from my chair, leaned over, and placed my hands on the gun and the magazine while saying, "Honey, why don't you let me take that and we can talk about what's going on."

His removal of the gun was hasty and fierce. He grabbed the gun and the ammunition, forcing the extra magazine back into his outer pocket while holding the gun pointed downward in his left hand. I stood fully, almost at attention, and prayed, *Lord, if there's anything separating me from you—remove it, take care of my boys, and help me be brave.* My position seemed ridiculous. An evident target from less than five feet away, and I thought, *Move closer.*

I moved around my desk with my hands extended, palms up, and sank to my knees to the right of his chair. The thought whispered through my mind, *He's right-handed.* Placing my left hand on his right shoulder, I reached for his right hand with my right hand, interlacing my fingers with his. "Honey, let's talk about this. Tell me what's going on." I had to think, let him talk . . . because I needed a plan.

✿ 6 ✿

The Strangest Passion

By April of 1999, I was completing my last maternity-leave internship in seventh-grade math at Sycamore Middle School. I had started the semester with a fifth-grade language arts and social studies position before moving to sixth-grade reading and science. By ending with seventh-grade math, I would have taught every grade level and every subject at SMS. As the school year began to wind down, summer loomed on the horizon and spirits soared as we prepared for the upcoming break. At some point on the day of April 20, it was brought to my attention that a tragedy was unfolding at Columbine High School in Colorado. By nightfall the world was flooded with news of the devastation. Along with the rest of the world, I reeled from the horrific story.

That night, sitting in bed, all I could think about was how two boys could plan such a terrible act without anyone knowing of their intentions. In the days and weeks that followed, I began researching school shootings—not for the gory details that much of the general public wanted to know, but because I was searching for answers. I was attempting to understand the unthinkable.

From that point on I began researching the history of school shootings and more specifically the young people (mostly teenage boys) who were responsible for these atrocities. Turning to professional journals and books written by mental health therapists, law enforcement agencies, and educators directly related to these acts of campus violence, I found myself more and more intrigued by the psychology of these perpetrators.

As the books and materials began to accumulate, I began to believe that there were patterns of trauma, mental or brain illness, or undiagnosed psychoses that were connected to these devastating incidents. I began to realize that perspective is always grounded in the reality of an individual. Many of us assume our reality is that of the majority, but that is not always the case.

Over the next decade I scoured graduate research, crime scene investigations, interviews by law enforcement, and even autopsies of mass killers, gathering every bit of information related to the topic of school violence I could find. My husband, friends, and many members of my family could not understand my dedication to this research. I honestly could not blame them. Why would a thirty-year-old woman want to study something so horrific and sad? I couldn't explain it; I just had to do it.

As 2009 opened, I created a six-hour training session for the eighteen school counselors in my county, titled "Recognizing Red Flags: A Counselor's Role in Preventing Teen Violence." This one-thousand-slide presentation was the culmination of ten years of research. Our counseling supervisor encouraged me to reach out to some of the law enforcement investigators we had befriended and invite them to attend. Just one did. Lt. Shannon Heflin, a father of two and the head of our Criminal Investigative Unit, agreed to participate. Little did we know his attendance would set into motion events that would allow me to share this training on a state—and, eventually, a national—level.

After the first training, Shannon came to me and said, "Molly, every person in law enforcement needs to see this training." He was so sincere, and he encouraged me to reach out to his training supervisor to see if we could train the entire force in our county—including our city officers. Shannon made me believe this effort was valid, and I prepared carefully, knowing this audience of toughened law enforcement officers would not be easy to impress.

I was right.

On the first day of training, I arrived early, set up my projector and laptop, and made a quick restroom stop to gather my thoughts and attempt to settle my nerves. Looking into the mirror, I wondered what these officers would think. Would they accept the opinion of a woman— not even in law enforcement, but in education—who had never faced the dangers they did on a daily basis? I remember saying a quick prayer as I stood there by the sink . . . and then I headed out to greet officers as they arrived. One officer in particular made it obvious he would rather be anywhere other than where he was—sitting in this training.

He commented sarcastically and loudly (knowing full well I could hear him), "I bet this one is going to be good."

For some reason this comment fueled me. These men would be no match for a woman who had spent ten years teaching thirteen-year-olds. I smiled, responding, "I'm so glad you think so because I fully intend to hit one out of the park." He grinned smugly and reclined in his seat, content to let me have that one small retort. Making eye contact with him, I was inwardly beaming. He had given me the challenge I needed.

At lunchtime, this same hardened officer approached me and apologized. I graciously accepted and told him that very often things are not what they seem. I appreciated his participation and the difficult questions he and the other officers had produced. Getting him to buy in brought others, and in the months to come, officers from surrounding counties and the Metro-Nashville force began to attend the trainings, too. I knew then that this information was valuable in preventing crime—not just investigating it, but actually preventing it.

God began to open doors, leading me to counties throughout Tennessee to share what I had learned. As the crowds grew, I thanked God for each person He brought to these trainings. I knew He had a plan for each member in the audience and that the information they learned might prevent a tragedy. Little did I know that there, mixed among the participants in various counties at various trainings, would be the men and women directly involved in the incident that would occur on September 28, 2016.

On that September day, every law enforcement officer who responded had been through my "Recognizing Red Flags" training. What was even more miraculous, however, is that every juvenile probation officer later assigned to this young man, and both juvenile judges who became part of this case (from two different counties), had also been through my training—some of them meeting me only one month before our incident when I spoke at a state conference for juvenile court in Memphis, Tennessee. Because of these trainings, these juvenile court and law enforcement officers all knew me personally prior to our incident. God had created and assembled, without my knowledge or planning, the perfect team of professional individuals to weather this storm. They were all allowed to bear witness. This was already so much greater than I could ever comprehend, and I had no idea that it existed at all.

❧ 7 ❧

The Battle

As he held the gun and I listened to him talk, I became focused on the bookshelf located directly across from me on eye level. It was there that I saw Danny. Danny had been a student in the last class I taught before transitioning to the counseling department. He had gone on to West Point and, upon graduation, his mother had sent me a picture of him in uniform. I had framed it and put it on my bookshelf. Danny had told me once that he'd kept the copy of Robert Frost's poem "The Road Not Taken" that I had given them in the eighth grade. Remembering this admission, I thought, "The Road Not Taken? This is more like the Road Never Taken."

During the minutes that followed, thoughts would appear in my head and exit through my mouth faster than I could process or understand them. It took me months of thought and consideration before I recognized that they were given to me straight from the Lord. I could never have manufactured them myself. Fear was crippling, but it had not rendered me immobile. The concrete tiling beneath the thin rug

The bookshelf I faced during the time I was on my knees beside the young man. The pictures of my children, family, and friends reminded me I had a lot to fight for. Danny's West Point graduation picture on the second shelf brought to memory "The Road Not Taken," as I reminded myself that my situation that day was the road never taken.

had caused my kneecaps to flatten. I shifted weight continuously from one knee to the other, curling my toes under my feet for support. The uncomfortable nature of the position in which I found myself was, surprisingly, a somewhat pleasant distraction. I remember taking note of the ring on the middle finger of my right hand—silver with a removable heart in the center. I had purchased the ring on a girls' trip to Indiana with my eighth-grade teacher friends. Two of them—Lisa and Robyn—were my current principals, and I thought about the fact that they were far away in the school office. There was nothing they could do to help me.

I realized I had nothing . . . no means of protection, no way to summon help, no defense. All I had was faith and the belief that God could protect me.

The young man felt he had three options: either he could give me the gun, he could "do something," or he could leave (I am unsure as to whether he meant the room or the school). He knew he had already committed a felony. He felt there was nothing that could keep him from going through with his plan. He had already shared that he had to kill people on our campus. He asked for the location of the SRO's office as well as the principal's office as he did not know the exact location of either. I responded to every question he asked with a question—a counseling strategy I had learned years prior and that, thanks to continued practice, seemed to be second nature during our conversation. I was struck with terror when he admitted why he felt he had to harm people on campus. I knew I was not dealing with an errant teenager bent on revenge of some nature. This child was in crisis. He continued to be agitated, confused, and scattered.

During this time he said, "Mrs. Hudgens, I came to you because I think that you're the only person who can talk me out of this."

"Well," I replied, "then let's talk about it."

We discussed his options, with me reminding him that even though he had brought a gun, he had not used it against anyone. I asked him to give the gun to me, emphasizing that removing this weapon from the situation would allow him to think more clearly. I felt that the gun was a distraction and expressed this to him. Each time I mentioned his

When Glenn looked into my office through the closed door, he saw me kneeling to the right of the chair in the center of the picture facing my desk and thought I was praying. I avoided eye contact out of fear for his life.

handing over the firearm, he would say that he wanted to give it to me but that he just couldn't.

The clock ticked in the background. To my heightened senses it sounded like a gong each time the second hand moved forward. Then, out of my peripheral vision, I noticed movement at my office door and realized it was Glenn. Something told me not to make eye contact with him. If I did, he might open the door and the mood of the room would immediately alter. I feared for Glenn's life if he disrupted the setting that had been created. To Glenn's credit, he moved on, returning to his office. I breathed a sigh of relief. In the months that followed I would ask Glenn what prevented him from opening the door. He told me he realized I was on my knees beside the student and thought I was praying. He noted it would have been unusual behavior for me, but something told him not to interrupt.

Every so often I would glance at the gun. How many bullets would the magazine hold? I remember trying to frantically count them and realizing that I could only see through the slit in the magazine. I guessed around ten. How many times would I have to pull the trigger to empty it? Could I fire it into the drop ceiling? What was above the ceiling? A steel roof. Could I take it from him? How could I ensure that I did not get shot in the process? What would I do, even if I did get the gun? Would he run? And, most importantly, did he have other weapons? I knew I was in the best shape of my life and that if this became physical, I felt I would have the upper hand. But what if I attempted to take the gun and missed? He would kill me. There would be no second chance, and then there would be no barrier between my office and our students. They would have no warning and no chance.

I had to keep engaging him in conversation. The thought came to me, *You're going to have to talk your way out of this. Just get him to give you the gun.* But how? What words could I possibly conjure up that would allow him to relinquish all power, to yield the upper hand? What could I say that would give him cause to reconsider? And what if what I said was wrong and angered him further or caused him to act impulsively? *Keep him comfortable. Relinquish power. Lower his emotions. You are doing this.* All of those thoughts raced through my mind, almost simultaneously. While those thoughts seemed to calm me, they did little to distract me from the obvious truth that at any moment he could change course.

Glancing again at the bookshelf, I saw the faces of my family. My grandparents, parents, children. I came from a family of fighters—strong men and women of faith. It was then, looking at them, that the most powerful message came to me . . . God's promise that He would later fulfill: *You will go home tonight.*

I knew "home" wasn't referring to Heaven. This was a battle, and suddenly it was revealed to me that God had been preparing me for years for this particular fight. A highlight reel sped through my mind, and I was in awe of the special circumstances God had given me in the thirty-nine years, 364 days prior to this one. I was about to experience a spiritual war, and with those simple words—*You will go home tonight*—echoing in my head, I took further strength from the following verses:

> For we wrestle not against flesh and blood, but against principalities, against powers, against the rulers of the darkness of this world, against spiritual wickedness in high places.
>
> Ephesians 6:12 KJV

The evil before me was not this child. This was a stronger force. One I could not fight alone.

But then I remembered this . . .

> No, in all these things we are more than conquerors through him who loved us. For I am convinced that neither death nor life, neither angels nor demons, neither the present nor the future, nor any powers, neither height nor depth, nor anything else in all creation, will be able to separate us from the love of God that is in Christ Jesus our Lord.
>
> Romans 8:37–39

As those words washed over and through me, I realized that as a mere mortal I had no power over this kind of evil, but the devil had no idea who I had on my side. As I turned my head toward the storm, I knew even if it killed me, I was protected. As long as I live, I will never forget the realization that I was far from alone.

As classes changed for a second time, I began to realize the small talk was losing effect. Dread sank through me as I realized too much time was elapsing. The counseling department was second only to the front office in terms of traffic, and it dawned on me that an hour had now passed, so it was only a matter of time until we were interrupted, unintentionally, by someone. I realized I urgently had to change course in conversation and say something that I otherwise might not have chosen to say. As the young man struggled with the weight of an irrevocable decision, he expressed the worthlessness he felt, and I began to sense a shift.

The change in his tone, in his wording and comments, catapulted me into the fear that he might attempt to take his own life. My research on students who had committed school shootings had taught me that many of these students attempt suicide or beg for someone to kill them upon being taken into custody. Now another scenario presented itself, and I prayed silently for direction. Would I allow him to shoot himself right in front of me? Would I try to stop him? Could I live with the memory of witnessing such an atrocity? My eyes burned with tears as I contemplated what to do. What to say.

Then, somewhere out of the silence, I heard myself say, "Honey, I'm not sure what it is, but I believe in my heart God has a plan for your life."

The seconds that followed were the most terrifying of the entire experience. He stiffened in his seat, shifted to look down at me, and then addressed me by name. He asked me if I believed in God. I thought instantly of Peter and how he had denied Christ three times. Then my thoughts turned to a student who was shot nine times at close range in the library at Columbine High School. She was in terrible pain and was crying out to God when one of the gunmen asked her if she believed in Him. When she responded that she did, they asked her why. Her response indicated that her parents had brought her up that way. Although horribly injured, the brave young woman survived the attack.

I thought of Matthew 10:33—"But whosoever shall deny me before men, him will I also deny before my Father which is in heaven" (KJV).

In that moment I knew that an eighteen-year-old kid at Columbine High School had gotten it right. With fear rising as if to drown me, I responded with the first phrase that entered my mind: "Well, honey, I do, but I feel like you don't. Is there a reason that you don't?"

He said he had asked for help many times and that God had never helped him.

Again, words poured forth as from someone else's mouth when I responded, "Well, what do you think this is, honey? God didn't tell you 'no.' He was telling you to wait . . . for me. I'm not sure what we're going to do, but I will not leave you, and we will figure this out."

He then told me I was a good person, but he was not a good person. I assured him that he was a good person. I said, "Rather than make a decision to harm others, you made the decision to seek help. I am proud of you for that."

Then he asked me how I could be sure God was real. I told him I could not answer for anyone else, but I could share with him an experience I had that assured me of God's reality. I asked if he would like to hear the story, and he said that he would. It was then that I shared the story of the "angel" who had visited me on the third floor of the Health building my freshman year at Western Kentucky—the student in the flannel shirt and jeans who had known my name even without my giving it to him. The young man listened intently as I talked.

Then he asked how I knew God could help him.

As his question filled the room for mere seconds, God began to reveal Himself to me in a mighty way that is impossible for my feeble human presence to describe accurately. I had an epiphany. He had mentioned God in reference to prayer. Then, he had asked if I believed in God, and how I could know that God was real. This had led him to ask how I knew God could help him. With these questions swirling, God created a way of escape I had previously thought to be an impossible option. An overwhelming gratitude poured over me as an idea formed in my mind. It was not a still, small voice, but nonetheless, there it was: *Offer to pray with him.* I had absolutely nothing to lose, and everything to gain.

With tears running down my cheeks, I said, "You mentioned prayer. Would you be offended if I prayed with you?" I was shocked when he told me that would be okay. Of all the things I wish I could experience again—could remember vividly—it is the exact words to that prayer.

I knew that God was my last hope short of attempting to try to somehow get help and risk losing everything if that was the wrong decision. Ironically, relief flooded me, and I felt rather indifferent to whatever happened next. You see, there is something about being resigned to your own death that gives you an unparalleled perspective on the present.

> *Whatever you have learned or received or heard*
> *from me, or seen in me—put it into practice.*
> *And the God of peace will be with you.*
>
> Philippians 4:9

❧ 8 ❧

Jo Byrns School: Student Teaching and Trusting God's Path

Upon graduation from Western Kentucky University in 1998, I researched schools close to home in an attempt to decide where I should complete student teaching. When I found Jo Byrns School, a kindergarten through twelfth-grade school in neighboring Robertson County, I knew that this was the place. There was only one problem: I had to be interviewed for the interim by the principal, John Mantooth.

I had never met Mr. Mantooth and assumed that a simple request to student teach at his school would suffice. I could not have been more wrong. When I contacted JBS and spoke to Mr. Mantooth, he told me I would have to come in for a formal interview. While surprised by the mandate, I prepared myself, drove to the school, and met a man who provided the most difficult interview situation I have ever experienced to date.

Mr. Mantooth was serious about education, and he was even more serious about the education of his students at Jo Byrns. At the end of the interview, he agreed to assign me to the tenth- and eleventh-grade English teacher for the fall semester. I was thrilled. Jo Byrns was similar in design and culture to the school I had attended growing up, and I immediately felt comfortable there.

To say that I loved Jo Byrns and learning under my supervising teacher—Miss Lynne—is an understatement. She gave me the freedom to create units on poetry, *Night* by Elie Wiesel, and *To Kill a Mockingbird* by Harper Lee. I practiced reading aloud at home in an effort to perfect the dialect. I knew it would make the story feel more authentic and show my students that I cared about the spoken word as well as the written.

I still love both of those books, not only for the content but because of the faces that stared back at me as I read. I wanted so much for literature to come alive to them, and there was great satisfaction in seeing that happen. We celebrated the students' successes and learned to appreciate different cultures and times in history. For me, it was the culmination of years of hard work, and I loved every minute of it.

During my time at Jo Byrns, I learned that a student had died tragically in a car accident the previous semester. One of the survivors of the accident, a young lady, was in my sophomore English class. I found that she would linger after class to talk to me as if she just needed someone to listen. While others struggled with how to interact with her about the accident, that did not bother me. She was processing the incident, and I didn't mind listening as she did so.

I also met a trio of the most unlikely crew of friends imaginable: Bennett was outgoing and prone to wearing collared shirts and khaki pants or shorts. Steven was quieter, more of an introvert with a witty personality. Then there was Kyle. The first time I ever saw him, Kyle's longer hair had been braided into tiny braids with multicolored rubber bands at the end, and he was dressed in JNCO jeans. For those of you who do not remember this fad of the late nineties, these jeans had legs that were large enough to hide a small child!

These three boys didn't seem like they would ever be friends, but they were, and their friendship had a profound influence on me. When I first met Kyle, I worried he was going to present as a "class clown" who would be a disruption or, at the very least, a distraction. I inadvertently judged him based on his physical appearance, but as the days and weeks passed, I learned he was a bright young man who brought great discussion to the class and was loved by students from all social groups. Kyle's lesson for me was not to judge a book by its cover. When my semester at Jo Byrns ended, the boys presented me with a poster of Herman Munster with a huge smile on his face. Each boy had signed his name on the character's forehead. When they gave it to me, Bennett said, "It looks just like you when you smile." I knew his comment was actually a compliment. That poster hung in my classroom for eight years and in my counseling office for two. Bennett, Kyle, and Steven taught me how to truly love kids.

My last day at Jo Byrns, I cried. It was Christmas and many of the kids brought me gifts—which I was not expecting. I kept every card and letter and still treasure them. Today I relish seeing the lives of those students play out through social media. I am so proud of their accomplishments and feel grateful to have played a small part in their lives.

When I left Jo Byrns, I finally worked up the courage to ask Mr. Mantooth (a man and leader I had come to greatly respect) why he had so extensively interviewed me before my coming to Jo Byrns.

He laughed and said, "Molly, you were the first person to request to intern at our school in twenty-five years, and I had to figure out why." I loved that response, and I told him so. Truthfully, had there been an open position at Jo Byrns, I would have gladly taken it. I thought my direction was to work in a high school setting, but God had another plan. Unbeknownst to me, I was about to become a middle school teacher.

> *If you remain in me and my words remain in you,*
> *ask whatever you wish, and it will be done for you.*
>
> John 15:7

❧ 9 ❧

An Answered Prayer

As we prayed together, tears poured down my face and pooled on my eyelashes. I was afraid to close my eyes, but his were closed—wrenched tightly shut. Words came forth, and I poured out my soul. While most of the words are lost to me now, I remember thanking God in detail for everything I knew about that child: his gifts, his abilities, and the loss he had experienced. I also thanked Him for bringing that child to me. The words "pound the throne of grace" washed over me as I begged God for help I could not provide.

In my notes I wrote, *I prayed for God to protect [child's name]—for Him to reach down right then and touch this child's heart and make this young man aware of His presence. I asked God to encourage him, to lift him up, and to reassure him that I would be there for him. I thanked God for this young man's life and for sending him to me when he needed help most. I asked God to guide my words and give me the right things to say to help this child, and I thanked God for giving me this opportunity to pray with him.*

We were sweating profusely, and I remember the taste of salt and not knowing if it had come from my perspiration or my tears. No prayer had ever issued from my heart with such fervor, urgency, or desperation as this one. I felt a pain in my back and shifted position slightly to relieve the pressure on my knees while trying to focus on every word.

At one point in the prayer, he raised the gun toward his temple. Every synapse in my brain began to fire and a metallic taste filled my mouth. My mind screamed, "No, God! NO!" as the realization that he might be about to take his life rained down on me.

What do I do, Lord? I prayed. *Do I attempt to stop him? Do I remain frozen and watch this happen?*

I silently pleaded with God to intervene as my left hand released the boy's shoulder and tentatively reached toward the gun. I would have to stop him. I could not live with allowing him to die at his own hand in front of me. And then I saw the barrel pass over his head and he absent-mindedly scratched his head with his middle finger, his index finger remaining on the trigger and the barrel of the gun pointing horizontally at me. Then his hand slid back down to its original position with the gun pointed at the floor, and sound rushed through my ears as if they were filling with blood from my pounding heart. Again, the insanity of the moment crashed into me.

It was then that the prayer culminated with the words, "Lord, whatever negative factor is affecting this situation, remove it from the equation." Every word was forceful as I choked it out—demanding, aggressive, and resolute. I tried to envision my childhood version of a devil being chased away from our presence. My shoulders ached and a sense of anger encased me. An overwhelming feeling of unexplained rage presented itself and was directed at an enemy I could not see. Simultaneously there occurred a rush of power I could not understand. In that moment, I knew we were not alone.

The enormity of what we were experiencing left me feeling breathless; I wondered if this young man could feel the same phenomenon. As the prayer ended, a sense of exhaustion filled me, and dizziness swept over me again. The young man's eyes searched my face, waiting to see what I would say next. There were no words coming, and the brief, heavy pause felt like an unending expanse of time.

He broke the silence by asking me what we were going to do. I told him that I had a friend in law enforcement, a man named Chris, who I believed could help us. I assured the young man that this friend would know what to do.

As he contemplated this option, he glanced up at a race medal hanging on the wall to our left. He told me he remembered that I liked to run. In that moment, I knew that God had prepared an opening. I told him that I did, and that I had run ten miles that morning before school, which wreaked havoc on the knees. He wanted me to return to my desk chair where I would be more comfortable, but I knew that too much time had passed. It would not be long before someone would notice my absence from my daily routine and come looking for me. So I said, "I'm sorry. I can't do that. I'm going to stay here as long as I have to no matter how much my knees hurt until you give me that gun."

Again, I glanced down at the weapon, still dangling helplessly from his left hand. His finger still rested on the trigger. Although I had asked him for it before, several times, and been denied each time, I asked for the weapon once more.

"Honey, why don't you give me the gun?" Each time I had asked for the gun previously, he had said that he wanted to give it to me but just couldn't. This time was different, and he and I both knew it.

He said he thought he wanted to give it to me, and again, God gifted me with the correct response.

I replied, "Why don't you just let me lean over and take it, and then you won't have to give it to me." One of the young man's greatest challenges during the course of the incident had been his belief about what would happen if he *didn't* harm people at school. My offer to take the gun rather than ask him to give it to me would allow the decision to be taken out of his hands and placed literally and metaphorically into mine. He nodded in agreement, told me he thought that would be okay, and reached over with his right hand to put the safety on.

Slowly, I leaned over and felt the coldness of the gun as I wrapped my fingers around the barrel and trigger. He slid both arms around me, and I embraced him tightly. We both wept and I held him tightly, hearing the words *Just hold him like he's yours, Molly. Just hold him like he's yours.* As a mother of two boys, I understood the command perfectly.

As I hugged him close to me with my left arm, my attention was drawn to the gun extending from my right hand—a gun I now knew was fully loaded just from the heaviness of it.

I am holding a loaded gun in a public school.

There was no way to rationalize or comprehend the significance of that concept.

Three minutes ticked away on the clock before he released me from our embrace, and I thanked God for the elementary teacher years before who had told me that if a child ever hugs you, you should never let go until they do. During those three minutes I would marvel at what had just taken place, thanking God over and over for His protection while saying to the child, "Just cry it all out, honey. Just cry it all out. You did what was right, and what is right is never easy, but it is still right. I love you, and I am proud of you."

That precious child had been standing on the edge of a precipice—about to slide over the side into forever darkness—and something inside him encouraged him to come to me. Even now I am humbled beyond imagination that God would allow me to be used in this way . . . to direct a child to safety in the midst of a raging storm. If the world had ended in that moment, I could not have been more surprised as I had just witnessed the greatest miracle of my life. How many people are gifted with knowing their purpose in life has been fulfilled? In those few minutes, I knew I had been forever changed.

Part II

The Process
and
the People

❧ 10 ❧

My Mentors in Education

*I*n 1998, with student teaching behind me and Christmas looming on the horizon, it was unlikely that I'd find a job in education. Unless a teacher resigns abruptly, it's next to impossible to find a teaching position in the middle of the year. My parents encouraged me to be patient and hope that a job might miraculously come open.

My mother, the office manager of our local newspaper, called me one day during the break and told me I needed to call Dianne Williams. Miss Dianne was the principal at the local middle school, and when visiting the newspaper she had mentioned to my mom that she had three teachers leaving on maternity leave—consecutively—during the 1999 spring semester. Was this an answer to my prayer? Really, Lord? Middle school? But desperate times call for desperate measures, so I made the decision to interview with Dianne. My interaction with her on that winter day would set the course for the remainder of my career.

Dianne is the only educator I know personally whose name is almost revered in our county. She was, and still is, a fearless leader, talented educator, loving mentor, and dedicated friend. She offered me a job that morning, and in the course of a day I went from being a high school English teacher to a middle school math, social studies, language arts, *and* science teacher. In the semester that followed, I would teach every grade and every subject at SMS while learning to love the staff and students in the process. Guided by Dianne's leadership and the miraculous opening of a seventh-grade language arts position the following year, I made the decision to stay at Sycamore Middle. It was—and remains—one of the best decisions of my life.

My mentors in education who have had such an influence on my life. Pictured left to right: Jenny Simpkins, Lisa Young, Robyn Miller, Molly Hudgens, Sherry Gibbs, Dianne Williams, Martha Moore, and Judy Bell (not pictured).

Under Dianne's influence, I soared as an educator. I loved teaching English, and, more than anything, I loved my students. I loved them as much as I knew how to love a child . . . until I had my own.

Teaching is not an easy profession. Creating lessons that would engage students while managing classroom behavior, dealing with unexpected interruptions, and navigating the social minefield that is middle school proved to be challenging. We read good books, and with all of the fervor I could muster, I tried to make even diagramming sentences a fun activity.

A few years into my tenure, Dianne moved to our school district's central office, and Judy Bell became our principal. Judy really should have her own chapter, simply because she is Judy. A fiery strawberry blonde who is constantly moving, Judy Bell is a force with which to be reckoned. It was under her leadership that I grew to become Sycamore Middle and Cheatham County's Middle School Teacher of the Year in 2005. Little did I know that the following school year would be my last in a classroom, because God had other plans.

During the 2005–2006 school year, two fights took place in eighth grade. Fights are not uncommon in middle school, when puberty and tempers can collide with violent outcomes, but one of the fights happened in my classroom when we were returning from a break, and it shook me. Later that year, another fight would involve a student being more seriously injured, and on that afternoon I found myself crying in the faculty restroom. I sat there in the dark and realized: something had shifted.

At the end of the year, Judy came to me with a tough decision. Our advanced language arts teacher was being promoted to principal at another school, and Judy was considering moving me into her current position. A school counselor was leaving at the same time, so a position in the counseling department was opening up, too.

I labored over my decision, and after spending time with a much-loved mentor debating the pros and cons, I asked her, "What do you think I should do?"

She responded, "I hear you saying that you're going to be Sycamore Middle School's next school counselor."

At that point I hadn't actually made the decision; I hadn't even realized I was leaning one way or the other. But this wise friend saw, or heard, something that I had not. After telling Judy of my decision, I then had to tell my eighth-grade colleagues. They were supportive and would agree to eat lunch with me the following year so I could still be a part of their group.

I credit Judy with knowing that it was the right time for me to make a change within our building. She allowed me to create my own counseling program, giving me the flexibility to be available to students as needed. By allowing for this design, I was also able to try new ideas, make mistakes, and grow as a counselor. Almost as soon as the move was in place, I knew I had made the right decision. Soon after that, Robyn Miller, my eighth-grade teammate, would become our assistant principal, putting into place the first half of the administrative team that would guide us so carefully through the storm that lay ahead.

A few years later, when Judy moved to our central office, Lisa Young, my partner in the English department at SMS, became our principal. Lisa is a consummate professional, and under her leadership, our school flourished. The team of Lisa and Robyn would see us rise to Level 5 status, the highest for growth on standardized testing we had ever achieved. This standing would rise in the midst of the most challenging year any of us had ever known.

These women created a culture at Sycamore Middle School that spanned twenty years and solidified our school as a "family." We may not have always seen eye to eye on every issue, but we love each other, and we love our students. It's that love and dedication, combined with the support of our Sycamore families, that uplifted and sustained us in the trial we would soon face.

Lisa retired in 2016, and Robyn was promoted to head principal, a position she still maintains. I am honored to have her as my leader and administrator, but even more grateful to call her one of my very best friends.

Sherry Gibbs, Jenny Simpkins, and Martha Moore, three more outstanding Cheatham County educators, also molded and influenced me through the years. Sherry was our elementary supervisor, and she and I were co-presidents of the Alpha Chi chapter of Delta Kappa Gamma—a service-oriented sorority for educators. Sherry's love for children and ability to be positive in every situation was a guiding light to me on more than one occasion.

Jenny and Martha were the administrative team at Sycamore High School during some of my formative years. They were such an example of leadership, and I will always be grateful for the partnership our schools were able to form during their administration.

Today, only Judy, Robyn, Martha, and I are still working in education; Dianne, Lisa, Sherry, and Jenny have retired. I am honored, on occasion, to get to have dinner with them and to know them not only as my role models but also as my friends.

❧ 11 ❧

Round Two

The young man and I released our long embrace. I stood up slowly as blood rushed back into my legs and burning began to race down both calves. I fought the urge to lean on the edge of the desk.

Holding the gun around the center of the casing, I said, "Why don't you go ahead and give me all the rest of it?" He fished in his outer pocket and handed me the additional magazine and the holster. Clutching the items to my chest, I walked around my desk and, using my spare hand, reached for the keys that hung from my lanyard. The smallest one would unlock the top drawer of my filing cabinet where I kept my purse.

As the key turned and the drawer rolled open, I noticed my handbag took up the bulk of the shallow drawer. I lowered the gun and additional items onto my purse, which caved in on one side to create a sort of cradle for the weapon. I thought, *I am putting a loaded gun on top of my bag.* The entire experience still seemed surreal.

I pushed the drawer closed and secured the lock, the keys falling back into place around my neck, and I experienced another elevation in my pulse. Before I could question its origin, another alarming thought coursed through my mind: *I have never heard of a school shooter with only one weapon.* Fear again welled up inside me as I began to consider the possibility that he might still be armed.

Rather than seating myself at my desk, I walked around it and joined him in the identical chair that sat adjacent to his own. With my knees only inches from his, I reached for a tissue and offered one to him. We sat and talked for another ten minutes. Our conversation centered on the problems he had been experiencing. The counselor in me still sought to help him find answers and peace. To anyone inexperienced in working with middle school–aged children, his issues would have appeared juvenile, simple, but to him they were serious and present. We didn't speak of what had just happened, but he was concerned about how his parents were going to react. Again, while trying to maintain intense focus, I knew that this was not the end. What next?

At this point he was calm and talkative, and I felt that the storm had passed, but the need to remain on high alert was ever present. I had to involve someone else, but how could this be done? My initial thought was that this young man was safe where he was, as was everyone else. If he were in fact still armed, moving him through the hallway between the counseling department and the front office was risking the possibility of encountering another student, and that could be a trigger.

If I used the phone, he would be listening from right across my desk and might react if something I said disturbed or irritated him. I would have to attempt to get a message to someone who could help me. My thoughts instantly went to Chris. "Officer Gilmore," as the students called him, was our student resource officer. At that time we shared his position with three other schools, so I wasn't sure if he was even on campus, but I had to make an attempt to contact him.

The young man understood that he had committed a crime and wanted to know what would happen to him as a result. I answered honestly, saying I wasn't sure. I had never actually dealt with an issue of this type before. Again, the thought of Chris entered my mind, and again, God gave me the perfect answer. I told the young man that I had a friend named Chris who was a law enforcement officer. Chris was

Sycamore Middle School's resource officer on September 28, 2016, was Chris Gilmore. Chris was a strong supporter of my training and joined me in Charlotte in 2019 to tell the law enforcement perspective of our incident.

a good person and would help us figure out what we needed to do. I asked if it was okay for me to contact Chris, and the young man nodded in agreement.

After dialing Chris's number, I counted two rings before he answered. The joy I felt at hearing his voice is indescribable. For the first time in over an hour, I was not alone anymore. Just this human presence on the other end of the phone brought an unexpected emotional response, and I fought to maintain my composure.

"Hey," I said. "I need for you to come down to my office for a minute."

Chris responded that he was in a meeting in our conference room with administration and a parent. He inquired as to my need to meet with him. With the child's eyes locked on mine, I prayed for wording that would not elicit alarm or panic on the part of the young man. Trying to appear nonchalant while attempting to will the urgency of the situation to Chris through my tone, I responded.

"Um, well, I need to talk to you about something that is pretty important. Can you come on down here now?" Chris explained that he would wrap things up and be down shortly. I hung up the phone, thinking I'd need to make small talk for another few minutes. I even got on the computer and went to our student management system. There, with access to his grades, I was able to itemize any missing assignments or work that needed to be redone—a task I had done regularly with many students.

Sensing that time was dragging and might be running out, I asked the young man if I could send a text message to my husband letting him know that our oldest son had baseball practice that afternoon. The child seemed surprised that I had asked, as if needing permission, and responded by granting it. Again, I wanted him to feel as if he had control of the situation and would not think that I was doing something underhanded by using my cell phone.

I texted Chris the following statement: *I have just taken a loaded gun off of a student in my office. It is locked in a cabinet. He doesn't know I am contacting you. Please come quickly.* As I pressed the button to send the message, I prayed that it would go through. Poor cell reception in our building had been an ongoing issue for years. The word "sending" beside the text box faded as the screen turned to black, and I hoped that it had gone through.

As the following minutes passed, I struggled to find conversational topics. My heart sank even deeper into my stomach as I realized Chris wasn't coming. Plan A had turned to Plan B . . . and that plan wasn't working either. Just as I pondered what to do next, the young man spoke up, saying he thought he was just going to go back to class. Panic seized me, and I asked to make one more attempt to contact Chris.

Rather than dialing his number, I dialed that of our assistant principal, Robyn Miller. Robyn was one of my best friends, and I intended to have a conversation on my end that would make no sense on hers. I knew she would know me well enough to know that something was wrong. The extension was immediately answered, and relief flooded me when I realized it was actually Chris on the other line.

"Heeeeyy . . . I thought you were coming down to talk to me," I stammered, knowing the child wasn't aware that it was Chris I had texted.

Chris said he had now moved on to investigating another issue and was reviewing bus video footage in Robyn's office.

Realizing that my attempt to express a sense of emergency was failing miserably, I said, "Well, I really need to talk to you about that drug assembly on Friday." Chris, puzzled, responded, "Molly, I'm not in charge of the assembly on Friday." Frantic to get Chris to find my message, I said, "Well, I think I sent you an email or a text about it. Will you see if you got it?" My heart plunged even deeper into my stomach as he responded, "I'm looking at my phone right now, and there is no message from you."

Seconds later, after Chris had responded that he had no message from me, I heard him say, "Well, there *is* a message from you!" My spirits soared, and I listened as he read from the screen aloud. "I have just taken a loaded gun off of a student . . ." Here Chris stopped reading and said, "Molly, stay on the phone, and I will be right there." Because he was unsure as to the current status of the student, Chris did not want the child to know he was already on his way to my office. He hung up the phone, and I continued to have a conversation with the buzzing dial tone on the other end saying, "Yes, yes, thank you. That sounds good."

Seeing Chris's face appear at the door to my office was one of the happiest moments of my life. I motioned for him to enter, and he came in calmly followed by another SRO, Jason Harvison. Jason, too, had attended my training years before and had been supportive of my efforts. Seeing him accompanying Chris was another blessing. Chris seated himself to the right of the child, and Jason seated himself in a chair behind the young man. As he did so, Jason mouthed words to me. I read his lips as they formed the words, "Where's the gun?" I turned in my chair and touched the side of the filing cabinet behind me as if checking the date on a paper affixed there. I then held up the keys on the end of my lanyard—turning them as if I was inspecting them before laying them quietly in my lap. Jason nodded, acknowledging that he understood the gun was locked in the cabinet and that the key to open it was on the lanyard around my neck.

Chris patiently and methodically maneuvered the young man through the events of the previous evening and the current morning by simply asking him to explain what had happened and responding with follow-up questions as the young man responded. I listened as he respectfully spoke to the young man, and my heart swelled with pride. Our Cheatham County law enforcement officers, who had endured being called "small-town cops" on far too many occasions, brought an unparalleled level of professionalism to interviewing the young man. After carefully ascertaining his story, Chris ensured that he had no further weapons. During the time that I had been hugging the child and holding the gun, I had not felt any, but Chris's search verified it. I felt my body sink into my chair with relief upon seeing that there were no other firearms.

When the questioning was completed, Chris asked me to follow him to the administrative office, leaving the young man behind in my office with Jason. As he closed my office door behind me in the small corridor of our outer office, Chris opened his arms and we embraced. He said, "You did a good job." Words of affirmation that I had done well. It was what I needed: to be assured that my actions had been acknowledged as positive.

We walked together to the front office, where I met with Lisa and Robyn. They were emotional, and I felt rather removed. In hindsight, it's easy to see I was in shock, but in the moment it seemed their reactions were elevated.

I remember saying, "Well, everything turned out all right." Realistic in nature, the comment seemed to sum up the event. It would be months before I would even begin to process what had just occurred . . . years before I could remember all of the details. But in that moment, I was relieved. The incident was over, and as the administration and office staff followed our crisis plan, Chris and Jason quietly and covertly moved the young man out of our building.

I returned to my office with an investigator, yet another officer whom I had known from my training, who also happened to have been one of our son's former baseball coaches. I used my keys to unlock the filing cabinet and pull open the drawer. I watched as he lifted the gun from where I had placed it on top of my purse. I was surprised to still see the gun lying there, as if it should have somehow disappeared when I locked it inside.

I remember being curious about the make and model of the gun but remained silent as the investigator removed it from the cabinet. I stood unmoving behind him. He dropped the magazine from the base and then popped a bullet from the gun's center.

I knew what that meant, but nonetheless he said, "Good God, Molly. There's one in the chamber."

I responded, "I know. I know."

I hadn't known, but then again, somehow I had. The gun had not only been loaded, it was hot, with a bullet set to be expelled with one pull of the trigger. As he placed the gun and the magazine of ammunition in an evidence bag, I remember wondering if I would ever see it again. What a strange thought. Somehow, it felt as if there was a bond between us—some bond between a human being and this inanimate object. It did not belong to me, yet I had worked so hard to get it. Now, someone with no connection to the previous hours was taking it away in the name of evidence.

I thought of that firearm many times over the course of the weeks to come, wondering what would become of it. It would take years before I fully comprehended that the gun and the child had somehow become synonymous in my mind. In the space of my office, in the quiet of that time, they both had exhibited a clear and present danger, but in my mind, they both were worthy of protection. I had risked all that I had, used every tool God gave me, and somehow, with His divine intervention, I had survived victorious.

In the absence of both the child and the gun, I felt an unexplainable void. Even in the winning, I prayed that not all would be lost. This child would still need protecting, and I resolved to fight as long as needed to ensure that he would endure. I had no idea what that would look like or even mean. I only knew this: I had promised him to see this through to the end, and I fully intended to do so.

It would be a month after the incident that I would see the young man for the last time.

The gun I would never see again.

> *They replied, "Believe in the Lord Jesus, and you*
> *will be saved—you and your household."*
>
> Acts 16:31

❧ 12 ❧

Jason and the Boys

I met my future husband in the summer of 1997 when my mother-in-law, Sandra, had a heart attack. We still joke that she had to go to such extremes to secure a daughter-in-law, but it was honestly her stay in the hospital that led me to meet Jason. I had actually seen Sandra's picture in my parents' yearbook, because she had graduated from high school with them in 1969. I didn't meet her, however, until her open heart surgery in 1997.

My aunt Kathy, who was still my favorite running buddy when I returned home from college on the weekends, asked me one weekend if I wanted to go shopping. She added that a friend and coworker was in the hospital, so we might stop and visit her while we were out. We did just that, and I had no idea that this kind lady would be my future mother-in-law.

A few weekends later, I met Jason when we stopped to inquire as to how Sandra was doing. Jason was cutting weeds at his dad's house, and when we drove by we saw him and stopped. He was so quiet and

My husband, Jason, and our sons, Bradley and Henry, are three
of my greatest blessings. Their support has been unwavering,
and the boys often introduce me at speaking engagements.

respectful. I remember Aunt Kathy teasing me about how cute he was.
When Sandra's health improved, she invited us to a fish fry at a campground on Lake Barkley. My parents attended as well and, while there,
decided to purchase a camper with Aunt Kathy and Uncle Buddy. It was
there, at Leatherwood, that Jason and I began a friendship.

He had a boat, and we would spend hours fishing, boat riding, and talking. It really was the best form of dating. Many weekends all of his family would be present, including his grandparents, who helped to oversee the campground. All four of his uncles also had campers, and we looked forward to spending time with all of them on the lake and at the campground.

Jason and I dated for four years before marrying in June 2001. He had bought a home the previous year, and after we married I joined him there. We literally lived five minutes from school, and I loved our neighbors and our home. We stayed there for three years before deciding to build a home on my grandparents' farm. It was there that we would begin our family.

My grandfather passed away just after the concrete footings were poured, and my grandmother asked me to perform his eulogy. Yet again, I found myself speaking publicly. While my father teased me about being the "funeral speaker," looking back, those experiences placed me in front of an audience. Paw was easily my biggest fan, and his loss in 2004 was one of the most difficult of my life. Rather than being nervous at his funeral, I found peace in speaking about him; looking back, God was preparing me for a future that would involve a great deal of public speaking.

Bradley was born the day before our sixth wedding anniversary. He had the same blue eyes as his dad and, as all babies do, completely changed our world. It would be five more years before Henry would join us and our family became complete. I was meant to be a boy mom.

As much as I loved the students I taught and counseled, there was no comparison to how much I loved my boys. I had never known anything could be so fulfilling as being a mother. With each passing year, the boys blessed me more and more with their inquisitive natures and outgoing personalities. Even now, seeing them at the end of each school day, bounding into my office, is such a joy for me.

On December 14, 2012, I was in my office when someone first brought to my attention that there had been a shooting at a school in Connecticut. I closed my office door and spent the better part of the day watching the coverage coming from Newtown—and crying. At 2:50, I found my assistant principal, Robyn, took her by the hand, and told her we were going out to meet the bus to get our boys off. We both had kindergartners. She agreed to do so but looked at me quizzically as I made the demand.

I remember saying, "We are going to meet our boys as they arrive because there are parents who will not be able to do that today."

I was devastated by every school shooting and the loss of life of the staff and students there, although I knew none of them. I kept newspaper articles and magazines about the events, and I prayed for those families. Today, looking back, I see that every school shooting both prior to September 28, 2016, and each one since has had a profound effect on me. There is just something about the violation of a school and its family—a place that is so sacred for so many—that breaks my heart.

The loss of any human life by a violent act is tragic, but for me, those acts linked to a school setting and students will always carry a heavier weight. Because of those losses, I make sure every day to tell my boys how very much I love them. They are the reason I exist, and every day that has passed since the incident at school is a blessing, because I get one more day with my family.

> *Trust in him at all times, you people; pour out*
> *your hearts to him, for God is our refuge.*
>
> Psalm 62:8

❧ 13 ❦

I'm Fine

As soon as I was back in my office, I settled in to write a statement for the sheriff's department. Then, I rushed off to get lunch for the officers assigned to our school. I remember vaguely calling my mother to tell her that an incident had occurred at school, and if she were to hear about it somewhere, she needed to know I was fine. At some point, I contacted Jason as well, though I have no recollection of that conversation at all.

After returning to school with the food, I spoke again with our administrators, marveling inwardly at their reactions. While they seemed emotional—obviously affected—I still felt removed.

I remember saying, "I'm fine. Everything turned out okay." Even today, I still believe the latter part of that statement, but I can see now, from the other side, that "fine" was nowhere close to my state of mind.

As the day continued, an all-call went out to parents, explaining that a gun had been recovered at school, and we braced ourselves for a mass exodus. Despite our concerns, only six students were checked out of school. The community we had built within our school families had created great faith in our administrators, and the recorded message from our principal, Lisa, assured them that their children were safe.

When school dismissed that afternoon, I stood at the front windows speaking to students as they boarded their buses to head home. None of them seemed aware that anything out of the ordinary had happened at school that day. Although we had been on lockout for the majority of the day, they never assumed the incident involved a direct threat to our school. I was grateful for their raucous laughter and naivete as they left campus.

We held a staff meeting where only the barest of details were given. Many teachers seemed emotional, whereas others were frustrated with the lack of information. I finally spoke, explaining that we were not sure exactly what we had the liberty to share but that when we had clearance to do so, more would be revealed.

I also said, "Every one of you needs to go home tonight and read Psalm 91, because we were not just afforded a hedge of protection today. We were afforded a fortress."

Leaving school, I headed to baseball practice with Bradley, and after returning home, I attended church with my family. In hindsight, I was obviously in shock. I was not fully internalizing the depth or breadth of what had happened to me. At bedtime, I was exhausted and fell immediately into a deep sleep. There were no haunting dreams, no tossing and turning. I slept soundly and awoke the next morning to run eight more miles as part of my marathon training. I had a routine, and I was following it.

Around ten o'clock the following morning, I learned that our sheriff, Mike Breedlove, was going to hold a press conference about the incident. I contacted my mother, who decided to attend incognito. She knew none of those in the media would recognize her or know she was related to me. It would be my mom who would contact me to tell me the sheriff had named me and called me a hero. She relayed the details of the news release and because of her years in journalism warned me to brace for what she believed would be an onslaught of local and state media.

She was right. Within an hour of the live conference we were contacted by a national news syndicate, and for the next week we were inundated with phone calls, voice mails, and emails from news media all across the country and even from Asia and South America.

I tried to determine the best course of action in responding to their requests, because it had dawned on me that any time I had ever read about or heard about a school shooting on television or in the media, another would soon follow on its heels. It became glaringly obvious to me that in order to protect my family, our school family, and our community, my best course of action was to deny all of their requests. Even though we had offers to travel to big cities to speak on national shows, I turned them all down. I did not need fifteen minutes of fame. I needed those I loved to return to normal as soon as possible.

I respectfully asked our staff to refuse any inquiries that came to them from media attempting to gain access to me or information about me or the incident. To my knowledge, none of them ever spoke about me to any of the press. Even now, I am so proud of and grateful to them for honoring my wishes.

The reporters were relentless, however, and chose to write their own stories even without my account. It was difficult to hear the erroneous comments delivered by newscasters who painted the situation as if they had spoken to me or even had access to what had gone on in my office. And for some reason, it infuriated me that they kept reporting "she spoke to the boy for forty-five minutes." It wasn't forty-five minutes; it was ninety minutes. I had watched every one of them tick by on my wall clock. Still, I remained silent.

Social media was besieged by commentators from all over the world who were weighing in on the incident. While the majority of comments were positive and encouraging, there were trolls who wrote horrific commentary indicating that I had had an inappropriate relationship with the young man. These comments were hurtful and infuriating. I longed to set the record straight and respond, but again, I knew that any interjections on my part would only fuel a fire that without my involvement would soon die out.

It was surreal, seeing my yearbook picture splashed across the evening news, and I was grateful to our local photographer for capturing an image that at least was flattering. Who knew it would be taken from our school website and used over and over again because I had no social media and no photographs of myself posted online? Other than calling the school, there were no avenues through which the media could gain access, and after the first week they stopped calling. After one had pretended to be a parent hoping to gain access to the building and others had camped out across from the school in a field hoping to catch a glimpse of me, it was a relief not to have to hurry to my vehicle every day when I thought the coast was clear.

On one particular day, I laughed with glee when I realized that our bus drivers had inadvertently formed a circle around the parking lot that worked as a shield from the reporters across the street. As I drove by, I watched them adjusting their ties and prepping their microphones to record their video segments. I was tempted to honk and wave, but I refrained.

Within an hour of the sheriff's press conference, we were contacted by the first media outlet that demanded an interview. When I requested time to consider, they refused and threatened to write and run their own story if I did not comply. This infuriated me, so I asked our director of schools to grant me permission to write my own statement and video record it in my office. I knew if parents could see me at school, they would know it was safe to send their own children. If I was not afraid to be there, then their children would not be afraid either. We recorded my statement—I wore my Life Is Beautiful shirt—and released it online. As soon as the world was able to see me and hear me speak, the media requests began to decrease. I learned from that incident that I never would allow the media to tell my story when I could tell it myself through avenues of God's design.

I stumbled through the next few days, unsure of what to say to staff and parents who were so thoughtful in their cards, words, and gifts. I was embarrassed by the attention and longed simply to get back to normal. I felt alone and isolated . . . and was not sure what anyone thought about me. It took a student confronting me to snap me back to reality.

He came to my office on Friday and said, "Mrs. Hudgens, are you guys going to talk to us about this, or are you going to sweep it under the rug and act as if nothing happened?"

I went to our principal and asked to talk to our eighth graders in the commons area of our school. There I gave them the opportunity to ask any questions they wanted to. We stayed there for almost an hour. I told them that this young man had done exactly what I had always asked them to do: In a time when he was struggling and knew no one else was aware he needed help, he stood in the gap for himself and came to me for help. I assured them we were going to close ranks and protect him. He had done the right thing, and we were going to be supportive while he got help and began to heal. I asked them not to share his name or make him the fodder for gossip. To my knowledge, they did just that, and his name was never released to the media or posted online. Every time I think of this class of students, I think about how proud I am of them for protecting this young man. Without realizing it, they were gifting him with a second chance.

But the tongue of the wise brings healing.

Proverbs 12:18

⤙ 14 ⤚

Aftermath and Steven

A few days after the incident, I was approached by a therapist on our staff, Steven Sellars. I had worked with Steven for years and had a great deal of respect for him. He visited me in my office and cautiously broached the subject of counseling.

He told me, "Molly, when you're ready, we'll find the right person for you to talk to." Steven already knew what I could not yet see. This was going to be a process, and I was in denial about the depth of my feelings.

I did not initially understand Steven's concern, but I trusted him enough to at least consider the idea. It became increasingly obvious to me in the first week that, with the barrage of media and social media, it would be difficult to find someone with whom I could speak openly and trust to keep my conversation confidential. My instincts told me there was no one. The loneliness was profound, but I resigned myself to absorb it. There simply seemed to be no other option.

In the week that followed, Steven returned, and I shared my concerns about speaking to a stranger about the incident. He nodded understanding, but still expressed his belief that I needed to talk with someone. I worked up the courage to ask him if he was willing to be that person. I knew it would be unorthodox, since those of us in the counseling profession know it's not best practice to counsel people you know. Giving advice to someone is one thing, but taking on the role of therapist is another. Nonetheless, Steven considered the idea and, much to my delight, agreed to work with me.

Someday I hope he will write his own book about his experiences working with servicemen and women in law enforcement, fire and rescue, and the military. God has allowed him opportunities to bless so many in our community, and his intervention in my life could not have been more divinely created. Steven knew that in order to process trauma, I would need the freedom to dissect every aspect of that day. He also understood that I would return to certain fears and fragments of that day over and over again. Patiently, he guided me through each one, peeling back the layers of every minute of that day and the days that would follow.

It is my firm belief that everyone could benefit from talking to a counselor or therapist. Too often we set aside our mental health because we cannot see immediate results and do not understand the benefits we will reap from investing time in the process. There were days that Steven would arrive at my door, and all I could think about was what I *should* have been doing instead. His consistent visits and methodical approach won me over, however, and I began to look forward to where our next talk would lead me on the road to recovery.

Steven is now working with veterans full time. Every time I think about that, my heart swells with pride. He has always had such a dedication to their health and well-being, and now he is making a difference in those returning from the front. Even after his job change, he still keeps in touch with me. This very book is a result of Steven's encouragement for me to put my thoughts down on paper as I moved through the weeks following the incident. Subconsciously, the English teacher in me had constructed my journal entries as chapters of a book. Without Steven's suggestion, this book might never have existed. He is a major reason why I am whole today.

❧ 15 ❧

Knights of the Round Table

I have always loved the story of King Arthur and his knights—the concept of the round table that allowed everyone seated there to be equal with the others on their right and left. All worked together for a noble cause and achieved much because of their dedication to each other. Our school mascot is the Knight, so honor, decorum, and civility are characteristics we strive to instill in our students. These very traits, among so many others, have been shown to me by the tightly knit group of friends I hold dear. If I had a round table around which to seat the knights in my life, it would contain the women who prayed and fought for me through the days and weeks following September 28, 2016.

My best friend base was already solidly in place with my college friends, Tracey and Cara, and my Sycamore friend, Robyn, when Stefanie Davenport arrived on the scene at SMS. Stef is one of those people who is positive and encouraging in every aspect of her life. She loves to laugh and spend time with her friends and family, and when you are with her, you just feel like the best version of yourself.

Our church family and friends at Friendship Church have blessed my life in so many ways. These women prayed me through the days that would follow our incident. Pictured with me left to right—Tina James, Heidi Owens, Amanda Durham, Holly Waller, Hope Flowers, Megan McNeill, and Dawn Shrout (not pictured). Hope is one of my former students and a reminder of the blessings received by being truly invested in the lives of students.

Stef, who has since moved with her family to another county, would contact me first that September morning at school, and at some point we had a conversation. Like the conversation with Jason, for some reason I do not remember it at all. What I do remember is the peace I felt upon hearing her voice. Somehow Stef could make everything right with the world. She had seen something about the situation online and wanted to make sure we were all safe. During the days that followed, I would expunge thoughts and memories to her in confusing bursts and random patterns. To her credit, she never faltered. Even as her father, a United States Army veteran from Vietnam, was losing his battle with pancreatic cancer, Stef remained a stalwart confidante.

Two weeks after the incident, Stef's father passed away and Robyn and I traveled to Indiana for his memorial service. Robyn, like Stef, held firm as I talked off and on the entire seven-hour trip about what had taken place that day. It was late at night as we drove a two-lane road through the country, and I shared with her the events and attempted to scrapbook cards and letters from people all over the country. Robyn said little, which is unlike her. She is usually the first one to offer sound advice or direction, but she seemed to sense that nothing was needed from her that night other than a listening ear.

It wasn't until three years later, at a conference in Las Vegas where we presented a workshop with Stefanie, that I would finally hear Robyn's version of the events of September 28, 2016. I was spellbound as she relayed the details of how she and Lisa had led our staff, students, and parents strategically through that day to prevent chaos and maintain order. Our students and their families had been protected by two outstanding administrators who led with quiet strength and careful decision-making, without any prior experience concerning an incident like this one.

Stefanie Davenport (far left) and Robyn Miller (center) are two of my best friends, and it was such a joy to introduce them to Medal of Honor recipient Chuck Hagemeister and his wife, Barbara, at the opening of the Charles H. Coolidge National Medal of Honor Heritage Center in Chattanooga, Tennessee, in February 2020. The Hagemeisters have been mentors and friends to me since our meeting in 2017.

Tears ran down my face, imagining our staff as each of them, in small groups in our conference room, was informed of what had taken place. Robyn described the emotion many of them had expressed, and the truth slammed into me that they had *all* been affected. This wasn't just a singular incident in which I was the only survivor. They had all held the line. Without questioning, they had followed our crisis plan, resisted their own feelings of fear, and without hesitation carried the students through the remainder of the day unscathed. We would all bear the scars of that day in our own way, but none of our students would suffer. As Robyn finished speaking, I remember thinking I had never been so proud of anyone. It is for this, and so many other reasons, that she would easily receive a seat at my round table.

In mid-November, I traveled to Bowling Green, Kentucky, to run the marathon for which I'd been training at the time of the incident. Seeing Cara at the hotel sent a flood of relief spilling over me. Again, this was a friend who had known me for twenty years. Even though we might not have kept in touch as much as we should have, we would pick right back up where we left off as if time was irrelevant. Only five weeks had passed since the gun incident, and again I found myself pouring out the event to Cara. Like Stefanie and Robyn, she too proved to be a bulwark of protection. Her realistic insight and honest interpretations of what I had experienced brought a new perspective to the incident.

Now, I speak with Cara almost every single day through phone calls, texts, or voice mails. She is definitely a kindred spirit, and when she traveled to Dallas to hear me speak at a conference, we shared a room just like in college. There is no one like CaraVan, and in terms of our proverbial table, she would be seated close by because her observations and insight are priceless . . . and terribly funny.

Tracey Bertram is without a doubt the most fearless, faithful, and loyal friend in the history of the world. Even though over twenty years have passed since college, we never allow more than a week or two to go by without touching base. On the rare occasions when our crazy schedules allow us to actually talk, we can chat for an hour without pause. In the days and weeks that followed, Tracey held me up in prayers and texts. I believe she would have left home and stayed with me indefinitely if she had not had three children and a husband who would have missed her!

If Tracey were seated at our table, she would pop up every few seconds to serve someone. It is her servant's heart that endears her to me in a way that is difficult to describe in words. She is truly a saint in her own right, and everyone who knows her can attest to her genuine, compassionate nature and willingness to always put others ahead of herself. I believe her reward in Heaven will be great and truly deserved.

When Jason and I moved to our family farm, we began looking for a church closer to home to attend. We found a church and a family at Friendship Church. It was there, in our Sunday school class, that the remaining knights were found: Heidi Owens, Holly Waller, Amanda Durham, Hope Flowers, and Dawn Shrout, and their husbands, rallied around me in prayer during the days and weeks that followed. Since then, our class has grown to include other women, like Tina James and Megan McNeill, who have offered me love and support as well. In those early days, however, it was those first five who would offer up daily prayers and comforting texts to reassure me of God's protection and future plans.

On September 28, 2016, Heidi texted me to say that whatever was happening at our school, she knew I had to be somehow involved. While I could say little in response, her sense as to the actual happenings going on at school could only have been gifted from God. The evening of the press conference, Heidi drove to our house and called me from our driveway.

She knew I might not want to talk, and said, "I just need to see your face." I remember hugging and hugging her outside by our garage. She only stayed for a few minutes, but that visit buoyed me before I returned to the living room to gaze in disbelief as my face stared back at us from the television screen.

Heidi joined me on Thanksgiving morning for our annual self-created 5K through her neighborhood. The "Autumn Amble," as we had named our run, took on a whole new meaning that year, as I had so much for which to be thankful.

Since that day, we have remained a solid unit. There have been many laughs and shared experiences through church events and outings through the years. We rally together through times of tragedy and pray each other through difficult circumstances. We are enjoying the years of watching our children grow up, and the best part is knowing that once they have grown, we will still have each other.

The best part of a table such as mine is the knowledge that there are always more seats available. God has brought some amazing Christian women into my life in the years since the incident, and I believe that before my life ends, more will arrive there. For all of those who are already there, and those yet to come, I am thankful. I may not be a king, but every day I feel like one, and that is better than all the riches this world could provide.

> *Consider it all joy, my brethren, when you encounter various trials, knowing that the testing of your faith produces endurance. And let endurance have its perfect result, so that you may be perfect and complete, lacking in nothing.*
>
> James 1:2–4 NASB

❧ 16 ❧

It Is Well with My Soul

The Saturday after the incident, I was slated to run a 5K for breast cancer awareness in Pleasant View in honor of my mom. We discussed that my attendance might be a distraction, but she encouraged me to go and pick up my race packet on Friday night in case I decided to run the following day. When I got home, I noticed someone had written "Hero" beside my name on the bag. As tears of appreciation filled my eyes, I slipped the runner's bib from the bag. The number that stared back at me in huge numerals was 91. Instantly I thought of Psalm 91 and my reminder to the staff after our debriefing the day of the incident to go home and read it. God had sent me a visible reminder that His protection was still present.

Amid the curious looks and whispers, I ran the race that Saturday. How could I not? My mom pointed out that my breast cancer awareness leggings had the word "courage" on the side. As I crossed the finish line, I ran to a barricaded area and sobbed. I was alive and that simple fact overwhelmed me. The number 91 has continued to surface in the years since as God's promise of protection continues to envelop me.

Fall break occurred two weeks after the incident, and our private lives had become a public circus. As people who had no social media and a small, tight-knit group of friends, we were trying to hide in plain sight. Everywhere we went to eat in our town, we would go to pay only to learn that someone else had already taken care of our bill. When Jason arrived at a local bakery to pick up Henry's birthday cake, he learned that someone had already paid for that, too. While I was so grateful, I was also embarrassed by all of the attention.

I didn't know how to respond to perfect strangers who wanted to embrace me or stop me in the middle of the grocery store aisle to thank me in person. I tried to look each one of them in the eye and accept their kindness with a heart of gratitude. I still couldn't fathom how anyone thought I had done something heroic. My actions were exactly what anyone else in my school would have done had they been faced with the same predicament. I was not special or more deserving than other educators across the country who had worked miracles in their own schools.

Jason decided it would do us all good to get out of town. We hastily planned a trip to the beach and headed south for a week's reprieve. I vividly remember the first day at the beach, as I was walking and picking up shells. A lady approached me and I braced myself for the shower of affection that was about to befall me.

She smiled and said, "I really like your swimsuit." I thanked her and continued on my walk. When she was out of hearing range, I laughed to myself. It felt wonderful. Why in the world anyone would ever want to be a celebrity is beyond me.

One early morning, I went down by the shore and wrote the date *9-28-16* in the sand. Then I had the best conversation with God I had had since the incident.

I said, "Lord, I want you to take this from me. I am not going to be a victim; I am going to be a survivor. I will not let this incident define me, but rather, I will define it. And Lord, in all things I will give you credit and praise." There, looking out at the ocean, it became clear to me that the God of the seas could navigate the waters I was set to sail. As long as

Two weeks after the incident, my family traveled to the
beach for fall break. There I stooped and wrote the date
in the sand and asked for God's protection and direction
in the days to come. He has never left me.

I knew the Captain of my ship and allowed Him to guide me, I would
arrive safely at every port.

This incident allowed my faith to solidify in a way that hadn't been
possible before that day at school. How could I have survived something
of this magnitude unscathed and not believe that God had saved me?
In the most desperate of moments, I was alone, but really . . . I wasn't.
When left with nothing but my faith, I had reached out to God, and He
had delivered me. Over and over that simple truth revealed itself. I had
not been alone. Kneeling there in that office, the very force of God had
been sent to shelter me. Tears ran down my cheeks as the waves lapped
at my feet. I had always known that God is our Father, but seeing His

personal protection of me as one of His children both overwhelmed and empowered me.

At the end of the week, we returned home, and I sent an email to all of our staff. The email contained only a picture of the date—*9-28-16*—in the sand. The subject heading said, "It Is Well with My Soul."

And it was, and it is.

Part III

The Present
and
the Progress

❧ 17 ❧

Cancer and the Medal of Honor

One month prior to the incident at school, my mom had been diagnosed with breast cancer. I still remember the day standing in my kitchen as she told me she thought she had seen a dent in one of her breasts. My mother, who had only been sick a handful of times in my entire life, could not have cancer. That just was not possible.

When she began the process of mammograms and testing, I could not and would not consider even the possibility that cancer would be present. Then, one morning I was running, thinking, and praying, and the thought formed: *She has cancer.* I dismissed it as exhaustion—dehydration from running twelve miles on a hot Saturday morning. In hindsight, I recognize the voice. God was preparing me for what would lie ahead.

The diagnosis of breast cancer was jarring. Although I had been forewarned, there really was no preparation for the news. My maternal grandmother had been diagnosed with breast cancer in August twenty years before, at the age of sixty-four. My mother's diagnosis would also fall in the month of August at the age of sixty-four. As she discussed options with her oncologist and surgeon, all I could think was, "She is a fighter, and there is no way she will lose."

During the months that followed, as she prepared for surgery, I struggled to discuss her medical condition with her. Years later, we shared with each other that her cancer had distracted me from what I had experienced at school, while my incident at school distracted her from all that she was going through physically. No one would have ever seen either of these incidents as a gift, but God knew what we needed to walk through that time in our lives.

In January 2017, I received a phone call in my office early one morning from a woman in Baltimore, Maryland. She asked me if I had ever heard of the Congressional Medal of Honor Foundation. I remember stumbling through some explanation of my knowledge of the Medal of Honor and was shocked when she explained the purpose for her call. She informed me that in 2008 the Congressional Medal of Honor Society, made up of the living recipients of the Medal of Honor, had created a civilian award to honor those who had shown heroism, bravery, or a volunteer spirit that went above and beyond that of those in normal everyday life. She went on to say that every year hundreds of people are nominated but only a few are chosen to become recipients.

I remember thinking, *What does this have to do with me? Has someone I know, one of our students or staff, been nominated?*

As if reading my mind, she said, "Mrs. Hudgens, you were nominated for the incident that occurred at your school, and you are one of nineteen finalists. If you are chosen, would you be able to come to Washington, DC, in March for the Citizen Honors ceremony?"

I was so taken aback by what she said that I honestly thought, *What incident at school?* It was as if my mind was in a self-imposed fog that had buried the events of four months prior. Then the realization of what she was saying sank beneath the surface, and I remember grabbing my planner and flipping to March.

My words stumbled over each other and, laughing, I said, "I'm not sure what I was planning on doing in March, but if I am chosen, I will be there." She laughed, too, and said she would contact me again in two weeks to tell me if I had been chosen as a recipient. I hung up the phone and stood up at my desk.

Emotion flooded me and I said, "Lord, wherever you lead, I will go. If you want me to go to Washington, DC, then I will do it. But, Lord, you will have to guide the way. This is already so much bigger than I will ever be, but if you want me to go and tell this story, then I will do it."

Sobs overcame me, and I sat back down in my desk chair, grateful for a private office and a place to process all that I had just learned. The Medal of Honor recipients . . . those people were American heroes. And some of them had read my story and thought it worthy of consideration for recognition. I had never felt less deserving of anything in my life. However, as the possibility opened itself to me, it dawned on me that God's story was meant to be told. Other than sharing with a few close friends and family, I had buried this story inside of me because I believed that was what was best for me to do. Jesus, Himself, had performed miracles that, on occasion, He had asked to be kept quiet. Truthfully, though, most who witnessed those miracles ran from town to town sharing them with everyone they met. Was this miracle of ours meant to be shared?

Two weeks later, Daddy and I would find ourselves in a waiting room in a Nashville hospital as my mom underwent a double mastectomy. Fifteen minutes into her surgery, I received a phone call from the lady who had called me the week before. I stepped out into the hallway to take her call in private. When she asked where I was and what I was doing, I told her about my mom's surgery.

She said, "Well, I hope I can bring a ray of sunshine to this day. You have been chosen as a recipient of the Citizen Honors award." As she obtained contact information from me, I fought to hold my emotions in check. My voice quivered as I gave her my email address, but I listened as she explained some logistics.

At the end of the call, I returned to the waiting room and whispered the news to Daddy. We both cried. I'm sure others in the seating area with us believed we had just received bad news. My thoughts flew back to my childhood and the devastation I felt at not even placing in that beauty contest. In high school, I even tied for and lost homecoming queen . . . twice. I'd occasionally thought, *I am not pretty enough, smart enough, thin enough, just not enough.* I had believed those negative things over and over in my life so many times. But I *had* been enough. God had made me enough, through no doing of my own. He had given me what I needed to be enough in that situation. I had never felt more special in my life.

When my mom came out of surgery and was waiting in recovery, she smiled when she saw us.

Daddy said, "Shirley, Molly has something to tell you."

As my eyes fixed on hers, I said, "Mama, I am going to be a Congressional Medal of Honor Citizen Honors Recipient, and you don't have cancer anymore. It is a red-letter day." We both cried. The news from her surgeon that the surgery had been a success had been the icing on the cake. God had delivered us both. My faith elevated still more as I praised God for his healing and blessings.

As my mom slept that evening, I went to the Congressional Medal of Honor Foundation website and watched the video there about the Citizen Honors award. I stifled my sobs as I read of the men and women who were posthumous recipients—seven of whom had died attempting to save students during school shootings. I knew their stories. I had read about them during my years of research. Their faces stared up at me from the web page, and as I moved from one to the next I whispered their names aloud. That night, alone in the darkness, I purposed in my heart to honor those men and women in every speech I gave for the rest of my life. Their lives and their ultimate sacrifice would matter. They were the heroes, not me, and one day on the shores of Heaven, I will tell them so. Until then, I wear a bracelet daily bearing their names and those who have since been named as posthumous recipients.

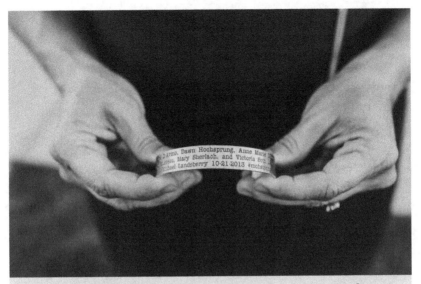

The original bracelet I had made bearing the names of the posthumous Citizen Honors recipients. I wear it daily, and each time another recipient is named, I have a new bracelet created. They are the real heroes, and as long as I live, they will never be forgotten.

Congressional Medal of Honor Citizen Honors posthumous recipients who lost their lives in their schools:

Sandy Hook Elementary School—Newtown, Connecticut— December 14, 2012
  2013 recipients
  - Rachel D'Avino
  - Dawn Hochsprung
  - Anne Marie Murphy
  - Lauren Rousseau
  - Mary Sherlach
  - Victoria Soto

Sparks Middle School—Reno, Nevada—October 21, 2013
  2014 recipient
  - Michael Landsberry

Marjory Stoneman Douglas High School—Parkland, Florida—February 14, 2018
  2019 recipients
  - Aaron Feis
  - Peter Wang—Young Hero recipient

University of North Carolina, Charlotte—Charlotte, North Carolina—April 30, 2019
  2020 recipient
  - Riley Howell

Santa Fe High School—Santa Fe, Texas—May 18, 2018
  2020 recipient
  - Christian Garcia—Young Hero recipient

❧ 18 ❦

The Congressional Medal of Honor Citizen Honors

In the months leading up to the ceremony, I watched every video vignette and read the story of every living Medal of Honor recipient. At the time, there were seventy-five. Each story was so overwhelming, and I cried each time one of the recipients mentioned his faith and gave credit to God. These men were living proof of Psalm 91, and God's protection of them on fields of battle astounded me. I vividly remember reading the story of one recipient from the Vietnam War, Gary Beikirch, who, upon completing his time in the military, had gone on to become a middle school counselor. He had the same job as me in the same setting as mine. I sobbed sitting in our bed when I read that story. If only I could meet him, I knew he would understand. What I didn't understand was that I desperately needed to share my story with someone, and it was about to happen in a big way.

In March 2017, Jason and I traveled to Washington, DC, where we met some of our nation's greatest heroes—the recipients of the Medal of Honor. I carried a copy of a book written about the recipients with me. Sticky notes lined the pages with my handwritten notes and thoughts on them. As we looked down from the plane, I reviewed the pages and wondered which I would meet during our time there.

The Citizen Honors ceremony at Arlington National Cemetery on March 25, 2017. Medal of Honor recipient Joe Marm has been one of many recipients who has encouraged and supported me.

On the day of the ceremony, several of us were asked to be interviewed by a local newspaper. During the interview I noticed two men enter the back of the hotel ballroom where the interviews were taking place. One of them was tall and stately with glasses and small streaks of gray in his hair. He seated himself within hearing distance of the reporter completing my interview. As I listened to the reporter's next question, I noticed the thin blue ribbon that adorned his neck, with a beautiful star suspended from its center. He was a Medal of Honor recipient. He was close enough that I could see his striking blue eyes. I forced myself back to the interviewer's question but felt that I should have been standing rather than sitting in this man's presence.

At the conclusion of the interview, the man rose from his seat and I felt my knees shake as I realized he was approaching me. He introduced himself and slid a round object into my hand as he spoke. Holding my hands as my grandmother used to, he told me what an amazing story I had to share. I lost all ability to speak as his next words touched my heart. He told me that this story was not mine. It was God's. He went on to explain that I had lived for a reason, and God was allowing me to be the storyteller of His miracle.

At that moment it became strikingly clear to me that I had come to Washington, DC, to get permission—permission to tell our story. For six months I had held it close to me, and this man, all of these men, were giving me permission to tell my story by sharing their own. I believe I stammered out the words "Thank you" as I looked down at my hands, too overwhelmed to even maintain eye contact.

Later, in private, I would open my clenched fist to reveal a challenge coin bearing his name—Roger Donlon. Vietnam. I had not even been born when God had delivered him from the enemy in a land so far away. He and so many others had carried the burden of their own experiences and were still standing even some forty years later. I realized these men had only been identified as heroes for their initial incidents, but truly, it was the lives they have lived after they became recipients that has made them heroes. Most of them support and encourage some sort of charitable cause. They have used the platform of the Medal of Honor to better mankind. I believe that each one was chosen personally by God for his encounters in war. Their obligation is to their fellow soldiers, their country, and one another. They are unlike any other people I have ever met.

The Citizen Honors ceremony was a three-day event that took place in the DC area culminating with the medal ceremony at a military base at Arlington National Cemetery on National Medal of Honor Day— March 25. I will never forget standing behind those men at the Tomb of the Unknown Soldier during the Changing of the Guard and the Wreath-Laying ceremony. I wished for sunglasses to hide the tears filling my eyes as I listened to the honor band playing our national anthem. My heart surged as I looked out at our nation's capital behind the sarcophagus and thought, "I have never been prouder to be an American."

Following the Medal of Honor events at the Tomb of the Unknown, we traveled to the site of the Citizen Honors ceremony. There, on a stage with five other recipients, I experienced one of the most moving moments of my life. Again, I felt undeserving, and as the weight of the medal settled, I thought about how so many of the recipients had shared that their Medal does not belong to them. It belongs to those who never came home. It belongs to those who gave the ultimate sacrifice for our freedom. It belongs to all of the families who had to face life without their loved ones. This was the "weight" of the Medal that they had described.

I stood there listening to the citations of the Citizen Honors recipients who followed me, but I was also thinking about those seven faces staring back from my computer screen: those educators who had lost their lives defending children. Immediately I recognized the parallel. Why had I lived when they had not? What was I supposed to do with the rest of my life? The weight of their losses surrounded me like a shroud, and I promised them again in that sacred place that they would live on. I promised to make them proud. These men and women who were strangers to me were my brothers and sisters in education.

And as I stood there, I thought, too, of the hundreds of students and teachers lost across our country in acts of school violence who would never be recognized this valiantly. Again, I purposed in my heart that somehow I would make a difference and honor all of them. From my years of research, I believed every person who committed an atrocity at a school was a person without hope. How could we find them before all hope was lost? And what could be done when we did? I prayed for God to provide an opportunity and show me the way.

Later that evening, we dined at the Library of Congress. My parents, our boys, and my aunt Kathy and uncle Buddy were able to be with us, and the day was made even more special by the fact that Aunt Kathy and Uncle Buddy's anniversary was that very day. As the photographer snapped one more picture of us with the Capitol behind us, I knew that again my life was about to change, and this time I would hand the reins straight to God. He already knew the outcome anyway.

❧ 19 ❧

Tennessee's Own
Mr. Charles Henry Coolidge

Upon our return home, I decided to try to find Tennessee's own Mr. Charles H. Coolidge, in the hopes that I could meet him and express my gratitude for his service. During my preparatory studying of Medal of Honor recipients before the Citizen Honors ceremony, I had discovered that Tennessee still had one living Medal of Honor recipient—Mr. Charles Henry Coolidge. I found the Charles H. Coolidge National Medal of Honor Heritage Center website listed in Chattanooga. The Heritage Center was a museum in a local mall that found a way, in a small nine-hundred-square-foot area, to display and honor the heroism of Medal of Honor recipients.

Mr. Charles Henry Coolidge is the oldest living Medal of
Honor recipient, the only living recipient from Tennessee,
and one of only two living recipients from WWII. The
Coolidge family welcomed us into their fold and continue
to be such dear friends to our family.

Nervously, I dialed the Heritage Center's number and spoke to a volunteer—Jim Wade. I blazed ahead, in one breath telling him the story of our incident at school and the Citizen Honors. He listened carefully, took down my information, and promised to have someone contact me. In just a few days they did, and we were invited to visit Chattanooga to tour the museum.

What an amazing day that turned out to be! Not only did we visit the Heritage Center and meet some of the board and volunteers, but they also surprised us with a visit to see Mr. Charles himself at his home on Signal Mountain. When I gazed into the eyes of that precious man, I knew I had met a kindred spirit. He was so gracious with our boys, and when he spoke, his eyes twinkled. Not only did we meet Mr. Charles that day, but we also met two of his sons, William (Bill) and John; one of his daughters-in-law, Marie; and a grandson, John Jr. That day was the beginning of a wonderful friendship between our families. They have embraced me as one of their own and have supported me in every endeavor.

I now love to visit Mr. Charles several times a year. To date, he is the oldest living Medal of Honor recipient, one of only two living recipients from World War II, and the only living recipient from the state of Tennessee. He is a testament to God's grace, and his faith still abounds. To me he is a giant among men, and it is on the shoulders of soldiers like him that our country stood during a time of war.

Today the Charles H. Coolidge National Medal of Honor Heritage Center graces the downtown district of Chattanooga. A new site has given it more space and the opportunity to share more about the Medal of Honor and its deserving recipients with beautiful displays and dedicated artistry. This iconic place is also an institute for learning, as teachers and students gather there to learn about the Congressional Medal of Honor Foundation's Character Development Program.

The Medal of Honor is deeply rooted in the state of Tennessee: President Lincoln awarded the first Medals of Honor for battles fought in the Chattanooga and Chickamauga areas. The first six recipients were Union soldiers known as the Andrews Raiders, who captured a rebel locomotive called "The General" and rode it north until it ran out of coal in Ringgold, Georgia. This incident would become known as the Great

The Charles H. Coolidge National Medal of Honor Heritage Center opened in February 2020 in Chattanooga, Tennessee. This beautiful museum and center for learning shares the stories of Medal of Honor recipients from across the country and offers students a place to learn the history of the Medal of Honor, which is deeply rooted in Tennessee.

Locomotive Chase, and most of the twenty-two men involved in the raid were captured. Eight were hanged and buried in the Chattanooga National Cemetery, where a monument is erected in their memory. It is only fitting that we honor this significance with a place that heralds all of our military heroes. The Heritage Center has done just that, and I am proud to serve on its advisory board.

One of the most precious gifts I have received is a place in the museum for the Citizen Honors. I am the first recipient from the state of Tennessee, and upon my death my medal will be displayed at the Heritage Center. It is my hope that many little girls who have longed to be a princess will pass the display, read our story, and realize that they, too, have the potential to do something that others will perceive as heroic. I hope that it will inspire them to believe in themselves and to strive to be a hero for someone in their lives. After all, who wants to be a beauty queen, a princess, or a homecoming queen when you can be a hero? Not me. Not ever.

☜ 20 ☞

The Shepherd's Men

The Citizen Honors allowed me, for the first time, the opportunity to spend more time with the military and veteran community. As I began to learn more about their service and sacrifice, I realized supporting causes have always found ways to recognize and uplift our servicemen and women.

I was unfamiliar with some of the staggering statistics associated with the personal cost of military service on veterans and their families. When I learned about the Shepherd's Men, I knew that this was a cause, a program, and a team of people that embraced all I hoped to support. This team of patriots is fighting to save the lives of our post–September 11 veterans.

The Shepherd Center in Atlanta, Georgia, is one of the most reputable hospitals for spinal cord and brain injury rehabilitation in the United States. Its special program, the SHARE Military Initiative, focuses on the recovery of veterans who have experienced post-traumatic stress, traumatic brain injury, or both. I had never heard of this

The Shepherd's Men, a group of veteran and citizen patriots, support the SHARE Military Initiative at the Shepherd Center in Atlanta, Georgia. Since its inception in 2014, this team has raised in excess of six million dollars for SHARE, which works to prevent veteran suicide. There is a 100 percent survival rate for SHARE participants.

organization or this program until I met the cofounder of the Shepherd's Men, Travis Ellis.

Travis also became a Congressional Medal of Honor Foundation Citizen Honors Recipient on March 25, 2017. We met on our way to the Citizen Honors ceremony, and when he learned that I enjoyed running, he told me I should join the Shepherd's Men on the Nashville leg of their run the following May. As I listened to him talk about this team who was fighting to prevent veteran suicide, I was shocked. I had no idea that twenty-two veterans take their own lives every day in our country, suffering from the invisible scars of war.

The Shepherd's Men team, composed of members of the United States military, veterans, and civilian patriots, run seven half marathons in seven cities over the course of eight to nine days along the East Coast, stopping at national landmarks and memorials, to recognize the efforts of the veterans who have defended our freedom for hundreds of years. These runs are completed with each member of the team wearing a twenty-two-pound flak jacket to recognize the lives of those lost each day. Their fundraising efforts, along with private donations, fully fund the SHARE initiative each year. To date, they have raised in excess of six million dollars and aided in saving the lives of over five hundred veterans. The SHARE initiative maintains a 100 percent survival rate of its participants, and some of the members of the Shepherd's Men team are graduates of the SHARE program.

This program and its team of special individuals have brought the importance of honoring and supporting veterans to the forefront, while also raising awareness about veteran suicide. We owe a debt to those who defend us both at home and abroad, and supporting programs like the Shepherd's Men are small ways we can give back.

I am so grateful for the support of this team that has allowed me to run with them twice now. Many helped me in the sharing of my story, like Krissy Williams, the team "mom," who has become a dear friend and supporter, and Miss Patti Reed, who encourages and lifts up so many while having experienced personally the loss of her veteran son. Their mission will continue to save lives, and it is my prayer that if there is a veteran who is reading this book who has found themselves struggling to deal with the experiences of war, they will research the Shepherd Center and learn about this life-saving initiative. Hope is not lost, and this team fights to save those who have fought so valiantly for all of us . . . until twenty-two is zero.

- shepherdsmen.com
- shepherd.org/patient-programs/care-for-us-service-members
- instagram.com/shepherdsmen
- twitter.com/ShepherdsMen
- facebook.com/shepherdsmen
- #shepherdsmen
- #until22iszero
- #SHAREtheburden
- #SHAREmilitaryinitiative

This chapter and poem are dedicated in loving memory of Matthew Gallagher, Michael Reed, and Rammon Macon.

"We Will Never Run Alone"

The shroud of fog that covers us
Lingers thickly in the air.
Grief rains down upon us
And anger simmers there.

A battle you were fighting,
When we could not see the war.
An enemy was attacking
For which we weren't forewarned.

We are struggling to understand
To make sense of what you'd lost
Knowing that we would have helped
No matter what the cost.

Yet now we try to face the future
While holding tightly to the past.
The memories you created in us
Must be strong enough to last.

Your laughter we will remember
Your heart we'll always know.
The longing for you won't subside,
But from this we will grow.

Somehow from the other side
You see what we cannot.
We must accept you've moved ahead
Beyond the pain we've got.

The sun for you will always rise
Behind a Crystal Sea,
Where trials faced by you on earth
Have now been forced to flee.

No longer plagued by injury.
No longer trapped within.
You've been granted eternity
Back where we all begin.

Reunited with some you've loved,
You've looked upon God's face . . .
Where time will reach forever . . .
And grace and mercy are commonplace.

For now, we look towards Heaven
To see you as you are.
Some days you'll draw us closer
Even when it feels so far.

Look down on us, our brother
For we know you are not gone.
Our dedication to this cause
Will boldly carry on.

The weight we choose to carry
Has much more meaning now.
As will the prayers that we will utter
Each time we humbly bow.

In the midst of deepest heartache
We will rise like never before
And you will cheer us on to victory
From sands of Golden Shores.

When we are troubled or in anguish
You will lift us ever high.
We will see you in the break of day
And across the evening skies

And when we run across the miles
For those we hope to save,
You will carry us through hard times
When we are anything but brave.

And every time we think of you
Resting there in Heaven's home,
We will know, that here on earth,
We will never run alone.

Molly Hudgens—October 2019

❧ 21 ❧

Sharing God's Story

As the year circled around, we began approaching the one-year anniversary of the event. During the weeks leading up to September 28, 2017, Robyn asked me, "How would you like for us to remember last year?" I had been thinking about it and decided that I wanted to be alone in my office. My plan was to lock the door, cover the window, and complete the scrapbook I had been making of the cards, letters, and emails that people had sent me. It seemed appropriate to reflect and think on how wonderfully I had been blessed in the previous year. In my heart, my desire was to take back that ninety minutes of my life, to not allow the fear from those minutes to define me, my life, or my future.

On the morning of September 28, I watched the clock as the minutes ticked by until 8:10. Then there was a knock at my door. I opened it to find our administration, some of our central office staff, and several of my close friends. They came with breakfast, and told me that they were there to help me "take back" those minutes of my life. As we ate and I looked around me, I saw again how much I had to be thankful for. By 9:50 they had all left, and I was alone in my office. As the last minutes of time expired, I internally celebrated 365 days of survival.

The next year, Henry was home with a stomach virus on September 28. As I stripped his sheets, he got sick again, and I hurried to put more laundry in and remake the bed. As it dawned on me that it was the second anniversary of the incident, I couldn't help but laugh. I realized the fear of that day would not be revisited every year. I wouldn't need to hold my breath for ninety minutes, fearing that something further may happen. Instead, the ninety minutes were spent cleaning up and doing laundry. God was ensuring that I was progressing, and He was providing healing.

The third anniversary fell on a Saturday, and during the ninety minutes, I went to the bank, picked up groceries, and drove home listening to a Christian radio station. Those errands are part of my Saturday morning routine, and I enjoyed the time worshipping in the car, listening to songs that had sustained me for the past three years. I'm sure some grocery clerks or passersby wondered about the tears in my eyes, but they never pointed them out. It would have been hard to explain, anyway, as they were tears of relief and gratitude.

Each year that passes reminds me that there is no need to fear any anniversary or any day, for that matter. God is already there, preparing a way and planning my footsteps. How grateful I am that I chose to relinquish control to Him. That decision is one I have never regretted.

Today I am still the seventh- and eighth-grade counselor at our school, and I love every day of it. My students bless me far more than I will ever bless them, and I am grateful to have been allowed to continue working at a place that is a second home. Aside from my job at school, God has gifted me with many opportunities to share His story all over the country.

Every time there is interest in my coming to share this story, I pray God will only open the doors through which He wants me to pass. When opportunities arise that do not work out, I just assume God did not desire for me to speak to those audiences. It is my sincere belief that every person who is present for the telling of this story was designed by God to hear it. When I look across a convention center or church or school at the faces before me, I often wonder, "Lord, what will You have them do with this story? How will it affect them, make them react, or change their lives?" The enormity of that overwhelms me, and most speaking occasions bring me to tears.

Before speaking, I try to slip behind a curtain or sit quietly in my seat with my head bowed and pray for God's direction and wisdom.

I always pray, "Lord, give me the words You want me to say." I also think, "Lord, when they hear and see me speak, please let them see You instead." The desire of my heart is to encourage hope in others, and to show them the love of God.

Carefully written speeches have given way to a few PowerPoint slides and me just pouring out whatever God lays on my heart. Those impromptu words have given me some of the greatest gifts of my life through hearing the responses from others. I have listened to hundreds of stories audience members have shared with me about events in their own lives, and I know that God is allowing them to share their burdens and heal us both in the process.

I have traveled to Las Vegas, Dallas, Charlotte, Valley Forge, and many other places across our country, and what I have found is this: It does not matter what religion you follow or denomination to which you belong. Your exact practices or specific beliefs do not matter. What matters is that people know the love of God. What matters is that they understand He made each of them specifically for a purpose that was individually designed. We cannot always understand His ways, but that's because we cannot see what all lies ahead. I believe that in the life beyond this one, He will answer all of our questions and reveal why things happened the way they did while we were here on earth. When we have the clarity of His understanding, we will rejoice even in the losses we suffered, the pain we endured, and the trials we faced. All will be made known, and we will be made whole.

God continues to move, and I marvel at how His tapestry has come to contain many of those who have experienced loss due to school shootings. In spring of 2020, I partnered with Safe and Sound Schools, a nonprofit organization created by Michele Gay and Alissa Parker—two mothers who lost their daughters at Sandy Hook Elementary School in 2012. Frank DeAngelis, who was the principal at Columbine High

School in 1999, is also part of the Safe and Sound Schools family. Only God could have taken three individuals whose stories I knew and for whom I had prayed and brought them into my life. Having the opportunity to tell them how their stories influenced my research and most likely saved lives at our school was an amazing blessing.

Until my life ends, I plan to continue sharing this story, God's story, with as many people as I possibly can in the hopes that one of them will come to trust in God upon hearing it. Even if it helps only one person, it will still have mattered.

> *A generous person will prosper; whoever refreshes others will be refreshed.*
>
> Proverbs 11:25
>
> *But this I call to mind, and therefore I have hope: The steadfast love of the LORD never ceases; his mercies never come to an end; they are new every morning; great is your faithfulness.*
>
> Lamentations 3:21–23 ESV

This Story Is Also Yours

Most people believe they understand school settings because they attended school themselves as children. The truth is that school, as we knew it ourselves as adolescents, is very different today. With changes in the world and society, entirely new challenges face those in education every day. Our students also face struggles none of us were exposed to as children. Social media, the Internet, and opportunities for around-the-clock social interaction have created on one hand great advances in technology and on the other . . . a monster.

Educators stay on the forefront of the changing tides in popular culture out of necessity and also because our students provide us with insight into the language, trends, and fads of their generation. Many of us believe we will learn, over the course of a teaching career, far more from them than they will learn from us. I know this is true of my experience.

I love my kids. From the first class of students I taught to the kids who are currently under my charge as a counselor, every one of them has been loved for different reasons. When I look back at my years as a classroom teacher, I know in my heart that the life lessons I attempted to bring to every class period were far more important than the sentences we diagrammed or the tests they took.

Over the years, I have asked many students what they felt was most valuable or most memorable about our shared classroom experiences. It has thrilled my soul to hear their responses and realize that very few, if any, are related to content material. The truth is that I was merely feeling my way through each year, trying to find stories to which they could relate and hoping that the example I attempted to model for them would be influential in a positive way.

Many students shared with me that they remembered how I read to them every day. Oh, I loved every second of every novel we read together! I wanted so much for them to love reading and to be passionate about it. We had engaging conversations in class about pieces we read, and they shared so much about their families. I treasured every story they relayed and every laugh they gave me. What I never realized was how profoundly these conversations were part of God's carefully designed training. He was giving me thousands of days to have conversations with students, allowing me to hone a craft I never knew I would need.

On days when my patience was tried, I learned that laughter would go much further than anger. One day I was fed up by constant classroom chatter when I was trying to present a lesson, and I walked outside of my classroom door into the outer courtyard and plucked a flower from the ground. I tucked it behind my ear and went back into the room. The kids were quiet—watching to see how I would react, as I very seldom displayed any signs of anger.

I sighed, smiled, and said, "Sometimes you just need to put a flower in your hair."

Students pushed me, molding me into a person who wanted their greater good, and they allowed nothing less than what I felt was their best potential. I trained them that "shut up" was a bad word and reminded them that "when somebody yells, nobody listens." Sometimes they would respond, question my thoughts further, or even disagree, but I knew that any of those responses meant that they were listening. I saw that as a win.

Those days of teaching allowed me to send a student possessing energy that needed to be dispelled out to run laps around the football field. It gave me the opportunity to practice punishing in private and praising them in public. They taught me, too, that a student throwing a paper wad might have been cause for frustration, but my reaction to his impulse would define his feelings toward me. I quickly learned that losing a relationship with a student was not an option, at least for me. Some days these middle school impulses would leave me feeling as if I did not like a child very much, but I never ever stopped loving them.

I was surrounded by thirteen-year-olds on September 11, 2001, during one of the darkest days of our country's history. Students would light a candle every day in my homeroom in honor of the soldiers who had been deployed to defend our freedom. In the years to come, I would visit Washington, DC, for the first time with a group of students. Seeing our nation's capital and exploring the monuments bonded us in a special way, and I still display a picture of one of those visits in my home. I love seeing their smiling faces, from all those years ago, and relish in knowing that some of them have children who now attend our school.

For each and every one of my students, past and present, I am grateful. I believe that every interaction I had with a student prior to September 28, 2016, was divine preparation for the most important conversation I would ever have at school. As I have aged, memory has not allowed me to remember the names of every student who has graced my path with his or her presence, but it is to them that I owe many thanks. These following words are expressly for them, and I hope they will read this as if I am speaking to them.

My Dear Students,

Every day when I enter my office, I glance at an end table beside the couch. On the lower shelf sit twenty-one yearbooks, and inside one of those books is your picture and your name. Some days I had to correct you, address your behavior, assign you a consequence for your action, and hold you accountable.

I did those things because I loved you. I loved you as much as I knew how to love children. I truly wanted you to make the most of our class and your education.

At the end of each class period, as you filed out of the room, I always concluded by saying, "I love you all. Have a wonderful day." I never wanted any of you to feel as if no one loved or cared about you. I kept every letter, note, or card you ever gave me, and those yearbooks also serve as scrapbooks that hold your graduation and wedding invitations, as well as the prayer cards of those of you whom we lost too young.

Some of you I have never seen again upon your completion of middle school, while others of you sit beside me in church each week or are part of our staff at school. Regardless of whether you are a current presence in my life or not, I carry each of you in my heart every day. I told you once that you would always be a part of me, and you have been. You will be as long as I am alive. There is no profession greater than that of a teacher. I had no idea that my investment in you would reap such amazing dividends, but I am reminded of that every time I see one of you and hear about your lives.

It is my prayer that you will love others as you have been loved and seek to use the gifts and talents you have been given by God to serve others. It is only in giving of yourselves that you will find true joy and happiness. For me, Philippians 1:3 describes my feelings for each of you. "I thank my God upon every remembrance of you" (KJV). May you be blessed daily and may God protect you and your families. I love you all. Have a wonderful day . . . and a wonderful life.

Much love,

Miss Bradley/Mrs. Hudgens

In the years that followed the events of September 28, 2016, I have prayed daily for God's guidance. I know that I am living on borrowed time to fulfill the Lord's will. He has a purpose for my life, and every day I have to submit myself to Him in order to allow Him to use me. If this story ever becomes about me, it will lose all significance. This story is about God's divine intervention and the deliverance of one person. It is so crucial that those who read this understand that God, too, has a purpose for your life. You are unique, created in His image, gifted with talents that allow you to serve and save others. You are already a miracle. What you choose to do with your life will reflect your Creator. When you are solidly in His will, you will experience true joy and know during every trial and tribulation that you are not alone.

And to the young man at our school: This story is also yours. I will always continue to be proud of you for making the decision that you did that day. I am equally proud that you are healing and preparing for a career of your choosing. It is important that you know I have prayed for you every single day. You are woven into the fabric of my life, and it was always my greatest hope that you would be given a second chance. I am so grateful that is going to be the case.

May you have a wonderful life full of laughter, family, friends, and amazing memories. And may you remind yourself—every single day— that you are loved. Your story, our story, has already saved the lives of others. Your bravery inspires those who are struggling to reach out for help. In this time in our world, when so many are missing the mark, you got it right. May everyone who finds themselves in a lost place find the courage to do what you did, and reach out to someone who can help them.

In 1994, at the age of eighteen, I wrote a poem that I found again only just this year. I cried uncontrollably for a few minutes upon reading it, as I saw the miracle God had performed in our lives prophesied twenty-two years earlier, when I was just the age that you are now. He always knew you would come to me on September 28, 2016, and that together, with His divine help, we would be rescued. I didn't understand what it meant when I wrote it, but now I know it was always for you, so I'm leaving it for you here. I hope it blesses your life, and I hope you will, in turn, continue to bless the lives of others. You were, dear child, created for a purpose, and I will always be cheering from the sidelines as you race to complete it.

"A Cry for Help"

You were only searching for answers
You knew you couldn't find.
You wanted someone to listen
And hear your silent cry.

You cried out for help in the darkness.
You found no other way.
If someone would only listen
Your life they'd be able to save.

But they were somehow too busy,
To stop and notice you,
There seemed no other way to get out,
There was only one thing left to do.

You had to get their attention,
And force them to understand.
The life they saw before them,
Was crumbling in your hands.

Then God sent you an answer,
An angel in disguise.
Someone who would listen
And share the tears you cried.

She was able to help you,
And enable you to see.
The life that you had been given
Was very precious indeed.

She offered her faith and her love;
She wanted nothing in return.
Your many trials had taught her things
She never thought she'd learn.

I've only known you for a short time,
But the person I've met is strong.
You've overcome so many obstacles,
And your cry for help is gone.

Your eyes now sparkle with laughter,
And a smile now graces your face.
You fought a good fight and finished,
The winner of the race.

God was listening for your cry,
And He heard when you spoke it that day.
He sent someone to help you;
He offered you another way.

It was all that you had been looking for,
It changed your life around.
Once just lost in darkness,
Now, you have been found.

May all of you who feel you are lost in darkness continue to search for light. It can be found. You are not alone. Always remember that even if there seems to be no one to stand in the gap, you can stand in the gap for yourself. Someone is ready and waiting to help you. The most courageous and difficult step you will ever take is admitting your struggle and asking for help.

Be brave. You are promised this:

"I am with you always, even unto the end of the world."

Matthew 28:20 KJV

If you long to know the God who protected me, you can find Him and His promises in the following verses. His gift of salvation is simple. All you have to do is request it, and it will be yours.

- Romans 3:10
- Romans 3:23
- Romans 5:8

- Romans 5:12
- Romans 6:23
- Romans 10:9–10
- Romans 10:13
- Romans 10:17

May God bless all of you as only He can, and if we never meet in this life, I look forward to the promise of Heaven and the opportunity to meet you there. In the meantime . . . #gobesomekidshero

Acknowledgments

This story, while mine in name, really belongs to so many. Within the pages of this book, the people who have most influenced my life have been named to show my love and gratitude. It is because of their effect on my life that I have been blessed beyond measure. There have been, however, many others who have supported me in special ways through the years, and for all of you who were not named, your contribution is no less valuable.

First and foremost, I am grateful to God for His protection of me on September 28, 2016, and every day since. His love and guidance have led me through many uncharted waters, and His daily provisions are more than I deserve.

God has blessed me with a wonderful family. Jason, Bradley, and Henry, thank you for making every day special and for supporting me during the telling of this story—which is also yours. May you know every day how much you are loved.

I am indebted always to the faculty and staff of Sycamore Middle School. My tenure there has granted me the opportunity to work in the presence of some of the most influential educators in our country. Their dedication to student learning and the betterment of children's lives is evidenced every day in their classrooms, and the example they lead has affected the lives of young people for many years. They have been and will always be my heroes.

I would be remiss if I did not thank, also, my church family. Friendship Church has blessed our lives for over ten years, and our pastors, Cecil Boswell, Dwayne James, Zach Vickery, and Kip McNeill, have prayed for and encouraged us through trials as well as triumphs.

It was there, four days after the incident, Bro. Cecil would allow me to share the testimony of September 28, 2016, wearing the same clothes I'd had on at school that day. Our Sunday school class at Friendship is composed of some of our closest friends, and they were crucial in praying for our family in the days and weeks that followed.

Much love to my parents, David and Shirley Bradley, and grandmother, Frances Milliken, for their support and dedication to this book, and to my heavenly grandparents, Harold and Mabel Bradley and Tillman Milliken, for the influence they had on my life.

My extended family is a network of support, and without my aunts and uncles, I would not be the person I am today. Much love always is given to Uncle Jack and Aunt Bonny Cannon, Uncle Earl and Aunt Jane Bradley, Aunt Dimple Bell, Uncle Don and Aunt Barbara Jenkins, Uncle Jimmy and Aunt Judy Bradley, Uncle Tad and Aunt Joyce Stone, Uncle Clyde and Aunt Sherry White, Uncle Buddy and Aunt Kathy Wright, and Uncle Ricky and Aunt Judy Harris.

I could not leave out my first cousins as most of my childhood memories involve one of them: Scott Cannon, Jackie Cannon Simpkins, Jason Cannon, Amanda Bradley Dee, Kevin Bradley, Karen Bradley Hampton, Kent Bradley, Kendall Bradley, Robyn Bell, Alycia Bell Mathis, Doug Bell, Brad Bell, Jeffrey Jenkins, Barry Jenkins, Donna Jenkins Yeager, Daniel Jenkins, Mark Stone, Jeremy White, Jamie White, Josh White, Derek Wright, Nathan Wright, Adam Wright, Stacey Harris Knight.

My in-laws have played a major part in my life as well for the last twenty years. Jason's grandparents, Sam and Jennie B. Austin and Clarence and Mattie Hudgens, have been such a strong spiritual support. Mr. Clarence passed away in 2006, and Mr. Sam and Miss Jennie B. passed away just eight months apart during the writing of this book. Heaven is that much sweeter because of their presence. Thank you to Jason's parents, Sandra Hudgens, and Randall and Golf Hudgens, for treating me as a daughter. Thank you also to my sister-in-law, Lee Ann Hudgens Honeycutt, her husband, Matt, and our niece and nephews, Aaron, Sarah, and Ryan, for their love and support.

I am especially grateful for Congressional Medal of Honor Recipient Mr. Charles Coolidge and the Charles H. Coolidge National Medal of Honor Heritage Center for recognizing the efforts of our nation's heroes—our Medal of Honor recipients. The Coolidge family has embraced me as part of their own, and their kindness means so much. Thank you to Mr. Charlie, Mr. Bill, Mr. John, Mrs. Marie, John Jr. (J. C.), Sara, and all of your family for the encouragement and support you have given to me and my family.

Thank you to the Congressional Medal of Honor Foundation and the Congressional Medal of Honor Society for honoring citizen heroes and for giving me the opportunity to share hope with others. To all of you—the Medal of Honor recipients—I give my gratitude for the encouragement you have given to me. You have the hearts of servants, and I am so thankful for your service to our country.

A special thank you to my best friends—Cara Adney, Tracey Bertram, Stefanie Davenport, Heidi Owens, and Robyn Miller—for being my confidantes and hiding place.

I'm especially grateful for Charlie Daniels, who read this book and provided an endorsement shortly before his passing on July 6, 2020.

To Travis Ellis and the Shepherd's Men, thank you for allowing me to be part of your family. Your mission to save veterans is making a difference, and so many lives will be changed in a positive way because you fought for those who were struggling. To all involved with the SHARE Military Initiative at the Shepherd Center in Atlanta, thank you for working alongside these families to allow true healing to take place.

To Dave and Shelley Burgess and the Dave Burgess Consulting family, I am forever thankful for the opportunity to share my life and this story with the world. It is because of you that I am able to do so.

Thank you to Lindsey Alexander and Mollie Turbeville for your guidance during the editing process and to Tara Martin for your tireless effort to promote and share this story.

I am grateful also to Michele Gay and the Safe and Sound Schools organization for allowing me a place within your family. Special thanks to our agent, Brian Regan, with Kirkland Productions as well.

A special thank you to those who read this book in its infancy and wrote such beautiful endorsements: Dr. Cathy Beck, Gary and Lolly Beikirch, Pat Brady, the Charles Coolidge family, Charlie Daniels, Sammy and Dixie Davis, Frank DeAngelis, Travis Ellis, Michele Gay, Chuck and Barbara Hagemeister, Dr. Peter Langman, and Bill Raines.

Special thanks to the amazing book team who made this story a reality in print and appreciated my love of grammatical accuracy. Our designer, Liz Schreiter; copyeditor, Amanda Kreklau; and proofreader, Nanette Bendyna, took special care in developing the pages and content of this book with attention to detail and symbolism that meant so much to me.

Thank you to Meri Crisp from Meri Crisp Photography for the yearbook picture "seen 'round the world."☺

Thank you to Maria Latham from Maria Latham Photography for the professional pictures and for your friendship.

About the Author

MOLLY BRADLEY HUDGENS is a 1998 and 2000 graduate of Western Kentucky University with a bachelor of arts degree in English and Allied Language Arts and a master of arts education degree in counseling. She is currently completing her twenty-first year as an educator in the Cheatham County School System, where she serves as a school counselor at Sycamore Middle School in Pleasant View, Tennessee. In addition to her counseling role, Mrs. Hudgens also currently serves on SMS's Crisis Management and Leadership Teams as well as sponsoring the Junior Beta Society at her school.

During her tenure in education, Hudgens has served as the president of the Alpha Chi chapter of Delta Kappa Gamma Society International and is an active member of the Honor Society of Phi Kappa Phi. Hudgens was also the writer of an NFL Play 60 Super School Grant for Sycamore Middle School.

After a personal experience in college, her interest in violence prevention and safety sparked a desire to educate others who work with intervening in the lives of potentially violent teenagers. Her in-depth study on school shootings and the teenagers who commit these acts, "Recognizing Red Flags," has been utilized nationally to train professionals in the fields of education, law enforcement, juvenile probation, and juvenile court. The training focuses on understanding the three types of school shooters and how to use threat assessment tools as an intervention to prevent violent acts in a school and community setting.

Mrs. Hudgens put her training to use on September 28, 2016, when she talked a student with a loaded handgun out of committing a mass shooting at Sycamore Middle School. Hudgens, the 2004–2005 and 2016–2017 Sycamore Middle School and Cheatham County Middle School Teacher of the Year, became a Congressional Medal of Honor Citizen Honors Recipient for a Single Act of Heroism from the Congressional Medal of Honor Foundation in March 2017. She is also the 2017 recipient of the Tennessee School Counseling Association's Phoebe White Award for Excellence in School Counseling and the 2019 Mental Health of the MidSouth's I. C. Hope Award for bringing mental health awareness to schools.

Hudgens has been the recipient of three state recognitions for heroic actions on September 28, 2016: a Proclamation from the Tennessee House of Representatives in October 2016, House Resolution No. 66 from the Tennessee House of Representatives in March 2017, and Senate Resolution No. 40 from the Tennessee State Senate in April 2017. Mrs. Hudgens has also been a nominee for the Carnegie Hero Fund Commission as well as the American Hero Channel's Red Bandanna Hero Award in 2017.

Hudgens is a member of the Professional Educators of Tennessee and the American School Counseling Association. She is also a treasurer and choir member at Friendship Church. Because she is the first Congressional Medal of Honor Citizen Honors Recipient from Tennessee, her story is exhibited in the newly opened Charles H. Coolidge National Medal of Honor Heritage Center in Chattanooga, Tennessee, where she serves as a member of the advisory board. Molly is also a speaker for Safe and Sound Schools through Kirkland Productions.

Mrs. Hudgens is the owner of Molly B. Hudgens Communications and is a nationally recognized motivational speaker as well as a violence prevention specialist. Molly resides in Ashland City, Tennessee, where she lives on her family farm with her husband, Jason, and two sons, Bradley and Henry. You can learn more about Molly Hudgens at:

Website: mollyhudgens.com
Twitter: @hudgensmolly
Facebook: Molly Hudgens
Instagram: @hudgensmolly
LinkedIn: Molly Bradley Hudgens

More from

DAVE BURGESS Consulting, inc.

Since 2012, DBCI has been publishing books that inspire and equip educators to be their best. For more information on our titles or to purchase bulk orders for your school, district, or book study, visit **DaveBurgessconsulting.com/DBCIbooks**.

More Inspiration, Professional Growth & Personal Development

Be REAL by Tara Martin

Be the One for Kids by Ryan Sheehy

The Coach ADVenture by Amy Illingworth

Creatively Productive by Lisa Johnson

Educational Eye Exam by Alicia Ray

The EduNinja Mindset by Jennifer Burdis

Empower Our Girls by Lynmara Colón and Adam Welcome

Finding Lifelines by Andrew Grieve and Andrew Sharos

The Four O'Clock Faculty by Rich Czyz

How Much Water Do We Have? by Pete and Kris Nunweiler

If the Dance Floor is Empty, Change the Song by Dr. Joe Clark

P Is for Pirate by Dave and Shelley Burgess

A Passion for Kindness by Tamara Letter

The Path to Serendipity by Allyson Apsey

Sanctuaries by Dan Tricarico

The SECRET SAUCE by Rich Czyz

Shattering the Perfect Teacher Myth by Aaron Hogan

Stories from Webb by Todd Nesloney

Talk to Me by Kim Bearden

Teach Better by Chad Ostrowski, Tiffany Ott, Rae Hughart, and Jeff Gargas

Teach Me, Teacher by Jacob Chastain

Teach, Play, Learn! by Adam Peterson

TeamMakers by Laura Robb and Evan Robb

Through the Lens of Serendipity by Allyson Apsey

The Zen Teacher by Dan Tricarico

Like a PIRATE™ Series

Teach Like a PIRATE by Dave Burgess

eXPlore Like a Pirate by Michael Matera

Learn Like a Pirate by Paul Solarz

Play Like a Pirate by Quinn Rollins

Run Like a Pirate by Adam Welcome

Tech Like a PIRATE by Matt Miller

Lead Like a PIRATE™ Series

Lead Like a PIRATE by Shelley Burgess and Beth Houf

Balance Like a Pirate by Jessica Cabeen, Jessica Johnson, and Sarah Johnson

Lead beyond Your Title by Nili Bartley

Lead with Appreciation by Amber Teamann and Melinda Miller

Lead with Culture by Jay Billy

Lead with Instructional Rounds by Vicki Wilson

Lead with Literacy by Mandy Ellis

Leadership & School Culture

Culturize by Jimmy Casas

Escaping the School Leader's Dunk Tank by Rebecca Coda and Rick Jetter

From Teacher to Leader by Starr Sackstein

The Innovator's Mindset by George Couros

It's OK to Say "They" by Christy Whittlesey

Kids Deserve It! by Todd Nesloney and Adam Welcome

Live Your Excellence by Jimmy Casas

Let Them Speak by Rebecca Coda and Rick Jetter

The Limitless School by Abe Hege and Adam Dovico

Next-Level Teaching by Jonathan Alsheimer

The Pepper Effect by Sean Gaillard

The Principled Principal by Jeffrey Zoul and Anthony McConnell

Relentless by Hamish Brewer

The Secret Solution by Todd Whitaker, Sam Miller, and Ryan Donlan

Start. Right. Now. by Todd Whitaker, Jeffrey Zoul, and Jimmy Casas

Stop. Right. Now. by Jimmy Casas and Jeffrey Zoul

Teach Your Class Off by CJ Reynolds

They Call Me "Mr. De" by Frank DeAngelis

Unmapped Potential by Julie Hasson and Missy Lennard

Word Shift by Joy Kirr

Your School Rocks by Ryan McLane and Eric Lowe

Technology & Tools

50 Things You Can Do with Google Classroom by Alice Keeler and Libbi Miller

50 Things to Go Further with Google Classroom by Alice Keeler and Libbi Miller

140 Twitter Tips for Educators by Brad Currie, Billy Krakower, and Scott Rocco

Block Breaker by Brian Aspinall

Code Breaker by Brian Aspinall

Control Alt Achieve by Eric Curts

Google Apps for Littles by Christine Pinto and Alice Keeler

Master the Media by Julie Smith

Reality Bytes by Christine Lion-Bailey, Jesse Lubinsky, and Micah Shippee, PhD

Sail the 7 Cs with Microsoft Education by Becky Keene and Kathi Kersznowski

Shake Up Learning by Kasey Bell

Social LEADia by Jennifer Casa-Todd

Stepping Up to Google Classroom by Alice Keeler and
Kimberly Mattina
Teaching Math with Google Apps by Alice Keeler and
Diana Herrington
Teachingland by Amanda Fox and Mary Ellen Weeks

Teaching Methods & Materials

All 4s and 5s by Andrew Sharos
Boredom Busters by Katie Powell
The Classroom Chef by John Stevens and Matt Vaudrey
The Collaborative Classroom by Trevor Muir
Copyrighteous by Diana Gill
Ditch That Homework by Matt Miller and Alice Keeler
Ditch That Textbook by Matt Miller
Don't Ditch That Tech by Matt Miller, Nate Ridgway, and
Angelia Ridgway
EDrenaline Rush by John Meehan
Educated by Design by Michael Cohen, The Tech Rabbi
The EduProtocol Field Guide by Marlena Hebern and Jon Corippo
The EduProtocol Field Guide: Book 2 by Marlena Hebern and
Jon Corippo
Instant Relevance by Denis Sheeran
LAUNCH by John Spencer and A. J. Juliani
Make Learning MAGICAL by Tisha Richmond
Pure Genius by Don Wettrick
The Revolution by Darren Ellwein and Derek McCoy
Shift This! by Joy Kirr
Skyrocket Your Teacher Coaching by Michael Cary Sonbert
Spark Learning by Ramsey Musallam
Sparks in the Dark by Travis Crowder and Todd Nesloney
Table Talk Math by John Stevens
The Wild Card by Hope and Wade King
The Writing on the Classroom Wall by Steve Wyborney

Children's Books

Beyond Us by Aaron Polansky

Cannonball In by Tara Martin
Dolphins in Trees by Aaron Polansky
I Want to Be a Lot by Ashley Savage
The Princes of Serendip by Allyson Apsey
The Wild Card Kids by Hope and Wade King
Zom-Be a Design Thinker by Amanda Fox

CPSIA information can be obtained
at www.ICGtesting.com
Printed in the USA
LVHW021238080521
686870LV00003B/155